ZAMBIA

TRAVEL GUIDE 2025

An Unforgettable Adventure Through Africa's Heart"

MCCLURE EDDIE

Copyright

© 2024 MCCLURE EDDIE. All rights reserved.

No part of this publication may be reproduced, distributed, or transmitted in any form or by any means, including photocopying, recording, or other electronic or mechanical methods, without the prior written permission of the author, except in the case of brief quotations embodied in critical reviews and certain other noncommercial uses permitted by copyright law. For permission requests, write to the author at the address below:

Disclaimer

The information provided in this publication is for general informational purposes only. All information in the publication is provided in good faith, however, MCCLURE EDDIE makes no representation or warranty of any kind, express or implied, regarding the accuracy, adequacy, validity, reliability, availability, or completeness of any information in this publication.

Under no circumstance shall MCCLURE EDDIE have any liability to you for any loss or damage of any kind incurred as a result of the use of this publication or reliance on any information provided in this publication. Your use of the publication and your reliance on any information in the publication is solely at your own risk.

This publication may contain links to other websites or content belonging to or originating from third parties or links to websites and features in banners or other advertising. Such external links are not investigated, monitored, or checked for accuracy, adequacy, validity, reliability, availability, or completeness by MCCLURE EDDIE.

MCCLURE EDDIE does not warrant, endorse, guarantee, or assume responsibility for the accuracy or reliability of any information offered by third-party websites linked through the publication or any website or feature linked in any banner or other advertising. MCCLURE EDDIE will not be a party to or in any way be responsible for monitoring any transaction between you and third-party providers of products or services.

Table of Contents

Introduction to Zambia

- Why Visit Zambia
- A Brief Overview of Zambia's Geography and Culture
- Key Travel Tips for First-Time Visitors

Top Attractions and Must-Visit Destinations

- Victoria Falls
- South Luangwa & Kafue National Parks
- Livingstone and Lusaka
- Off-the-Beaten-Path Destinations
- Unique Experiences and Hidden Gems

Zambian Cuisine and Dining

- Traditional Zambian Dishes
- Recommended Restaurants and Local Dining Spots
- International Cuisine Options in Zambia

Accommodation and Recommended Hotels

- Luxury, Mid-Range, and Budget Options
- Unique Stays: Eco-Lodges, Camping, and Cultural Lodging

- Top Hotels: Royal Livingstone, InterContinental Lusaka, and More

Practical Travel Information

- Transportation: Getting Around Zambia
- Currency, Banks, and ATMs
- Car Rentals and Driving Tips
- Emergency Contacts and Local Safety Guidelines

Cultural Insights and Local Customs

- Zambia's Cultural Etiquette
- Festivals, Traditions, and Social Norms
- Language Guide and Communication Tips

Sample Itinerary and Travel Planning

- 7-10 Day Adventure Itinerary
- Best Times to Visit Zambia
- What to Pack and Health Tips
- Contact Information for Hotels, Restaurants, and Tourist Assistance

CHAPTER ONE

Introduction to Zambia

Why Visit Zambia

Zambia, often regarded as one of Africa's hidden gems, offers a unique blend of natural beauty, rich culture, and thrilling adventures. Whether you are a nature enthusiast, an adrenaline seeker, or someone interested in experiencing authentic African culture, Zambia has something to offer. Here's why Zambia should be at the top of your travel list:

Victoria Falls

Zambia is home to one of the Seven Natural Wonders of the World: **Victoria Falls**, one of the largest and most spectacular waterfalls on Earth. The sight and sound of millions of gallons of water cascading over a cliff create a truly awe-inspiring experience. The nearby town of Livingstone provides easy access to the falls, making it a must-visit destination.

World-Class Safari Experiences

Zambia's national parks, including **South Luangwa** and **Kafue**, offer some of the best safari experiences in Africa. Known for its walking safaris, Zambia allows you to explore the wilderness up close and personal, guided by expert rangers. These parks are home to an abundance of wildlife, including lions, elephants, leopards, and the rare wild dog.

Diverse Wildlife and Nature

Beyond safaris, Zambia boasts stunning landscapes such as the **Lower Zambezi National Park**, the **Bangweulu Wetlands**, and **Lake Tanganyika**. These sites are perfect for nature lovers and bird watchers, offering a chance to see diverse ecosystems, from riverbanks and wetlands to dense forests and savannas.

Authentic Cultural Experiences

Zambia is home to over 70 ethnic groups, each with its own unique traditions, customs, and festivals. Visitors can engage with local communities, learn about traditional ceremonies, and even witness the vibrant celebrations during events like the **Kuomboka Festival** or the **Nsama Festival**.

Adventure Activities

Zambia is a haven for adventure seekers. From bungee jumping off the **Victoria Falls Bridge** to white-water rafting on the Zambezi River, there's no shortage of heart-pounding activities. Additionally, kayaking, fishing, and scenic flights over the falls offer unparalleled views and experiences.

Unspoiled, Less Crowded Destinations

Unlike other popular African destinations, Zambia remains relatively untouched by mass tourism, giving you the chance to explore its natural wonders without large crowds. This creates a more intimate, serene experience in some of the continent's most pristine environments.

Warm Zambian Hospitality

Zambians are known for their friendly, welcoming nature. The country's relaxed atmosphere, combined with its people's genuine hospitality, makes every visitor feel at home. Whether you're in the bustling capital city of Lusaka or a remote safari lodge, the warmth of the Zambian people will leave a lasting impression.

In summary, Zambia offers a perfect blend of natural wonders, wildlife, adventure, and culture. Whether you're exploring the majesty of Victoria Falls, embarking on a thrilling safari, or immersing yourself in the rich traditions of the local communities, Zambia promises an unforgettable experience for every traveler.

A Brief Overview of Zambia's Geography and Culture

Geography:

Located in the heart of southern Africa, **Zambia** is a landlocked country bordered by eight countries: **Tanzania** to the northeast, **Malawi** to the east, **Mozambique** to the southeast, **Zimbabwe** to the south, **Botswana** and **Namibia** to the southwest, and **Angola** to the northwest. With an area of approximately **752,612 square kilometers**, Zambia is slightly larger than the state of Texas, offering a diverse range of landscapes from vast savannahs and wetlands to rolling plateaus and dense forests.

The country is divided into three major regions:

The Zambezi River Basin

- Home to the iconic **Victoria Falls**, the Zambezi River is a significant waterway in Zambia and forms part of its southern border. It is the fourth-longest river in

Africa and supports various national parks and reserves along its course.

The Central Plateau

- This expansive plateau is the country's heartland and features a mix of grasslands, forests, and fertile farmland. The plateau is dotted with Zambia's major cities, including the capital, **Lusaka**.

The Copperbelt Region

- Located in the northwest, this region is rich in mineral resources, particularly copper, which has been the foundation of Zambia's economy for decades.
- Zambia is also known for its **national parks** and **wildlife reserves**, making it a premier destination for safaris. The country's diverse ecosystems provide homes for over 200 mammal species, including elephants, lions, leopards, and rare species like the wild dog.

Climate:

- Zambia experiences a **tropical climate**, characterized by a rainy season from November to April and a dry season from May to October. Temperatures range from **mild** to **warm**, with cooler weather at higher elevations, particularly in the central and northern regions.

Culture:

- Zambia is a culturally rich and diverse country, with over **70 distinct ethnic groups**, each contributing to the country's vibrant cultural fabric. The major ethnic groups include the **Bemba**, **Nyanja**, **Lozi**, **Tonga**, and **Chewa**, among others. This diversity is reflected in Zambia's language, traditions, and customs.

Language:

- The official language of Zambia is **English**, a legacy of its colonial history. However, **Bemba**, **Nyanja**, **Tonga**, and **Lozi** are among the most widely spoken local languages, with each region having its own dominant language. Zambians are generally multilingual, speaking several languages fluently.

Traditions and Festivals:

Zambia is known for its strong cultural traditions, many of which are celebrated through music, dance, and festivals. Some of the most notable festivals include:

- **Kuomboka Festival**: Celebrated by the Lozi people, this festival marks the annual migration of the king's people from the floodplains to higher ground.
- **Nsama Festival**: Celebrated by the Bemba people, it features traditional dances, songs, and rituals to honor ancestors and promote community unity.
- **N'cwala Festival**: A cultural festival held by the Ngoni people to celebrate the harvest and honor their chief.

Traditional **music and dance** are integral parts of Zambian life, and performances are often seen during celebrations, ceremonies, and in village gatherings. **Drums, rattles, and flutes** are commonly used in musical performances, with each ethnic group having its unique style of music and dance.

Food and Cuisine:

- Zambian cuisine is largely based on **maize**, which is used to make **nshima**, the staple food of the country. Nshima is often served with a variety of accompaniments such as vegetables, meat stews, and fish. Other popular dishes include **chikanda** (a type of meatloaf made with wild roots), **ifishimu** (grilled fish), and **isombe** (steamed cassava leaves). Street food such as **samp, boiled maize**, and **samosas** is commonly enjoyed by locals and visitors alike.

Art and Craftsmanship:

- Zambia's artistic heritage is reflected in its **handmade crafts**, including **wood carvings**, **pottery**, **beaded jewelry**, and **woven baskets**. Many of these crafts are produced by local artisans and are often sold in markets and villages, offering a glimpse into the rich artistic traditions of the various ethnic groups.

Religious Beliefs:

- Christianity is the dominant religion in Zambia, with the majority of Zambians identifying as Christians. Traditional African beliefs, however, still play a significant role in the daily lives of many Zambians, with various rituals and ceremonies honoring ancestors and spiritual forces. **Islam** and **Hinduism** also have small communities within the country, especially in urban areas.

In summary, Zambia's geography and culture offer a wealth of experiences for visitors. From its stunning natural beauty and rich wildlife to its diverse ethnic traditions and welcoming people, Zambia provides an unforgettable adventure steeped in both nature and culture.

Key Travel Tips for First-Time Visitors

Visiting Zambia is an exciting adventure, but like any international destination, it's important to be well-prepared. Here are some essential travel tips to ensure a smooth and enjoyable trip:

Visa Requirements

Most visitors to Zambia require a visa. Citizens of many countries, including the US, UK, Canada, and most EU nations, can obtain a visa on arrival, but it's recommended to check specific requirements well in advance. Travelers can also apply for an e-Visa through Zambia's official visa portal for convenience.

Health and Vaccinations

- **Vaccinations**: It's important to visit a healthcare professional before traveling to ensure you're up to date on required vaccinations, such as **yellow fever**, **hepatitis A and B**, and **typhoid**.
- **Malaria**: Zambia is a malaria-endemic country, especially in the rainy season (November to April). Carry mosquito repellent, sleep under a mosquito net, and

17

take antimalarial medication if recommended by your doctor.
- **Travel Insurance**: Always purchase comprehensive travel insurance that covers medical expenses, including emergency evacuation.

Money and Currency

The official currency in Zambia is the **Zambian Kwacha (ZMK)**.

- **ATMs**: ATMs are widely available in major cities like Lusaka and Livingstone. However, they might not be available in rural areas, so plan ahead and carry enough cash for your trips to remote locations.
- **Credit Cards**: Major credit cards (Visa, MasterCard) are accepted in larger hotels, restaurants, and shops, but small businesses may prefer cash. It's advisable to inform your bank of your travel plans to avoid any issues with card payments.
- **Currency Exchange**: Currency exchange is available at banks, airports, and exchange bureaus. Rates are better in cities than at airports.

Local Transportation

- **Public Transport**: Public transport in Zambia includes buses and minibus taxis, though they can be crowded and unreliable, especially in rural areas.
- **Car Rentals**: Renting a car is a popular way to get around, especially for safaris or exploring national parks. Ensure you have an international driving permit and familiarize yourself with local driving laws (driving is on the left).
- **Taxis and Ride-Hailing**: In major cities, taxis and ride-hailing apps like Uber and Bolt are available. Always confirm fares before starting a trip.
- **Domestic Flights**: Zambia has a few internal flights connecting major cities and tourist destinations. Book in advance to secure better rates.
- **Safety and Security**
  Zambia is generally a safe country for tourists, but like any destination, it's important to take precautions:
- **Personal Belongings**: Keep your valuables secure, especially in crowded places and public transport. Use hotel safes where available.

- **Street Safety**: Exercise caution at night, especially in large cities like Lusaka. Avoid walking alone in poorly lit areas.
- **Wildlife Safety**: When visiting national parks or wildlife reserves, always follow the guidelines provided by your tour guide to stay safe. Never approach wildlife, especially large animals like elephants and lions.

Local Etiquette and Customs

- **Greetings**: Zambians are friendly and polite. Greetings are an important part of the culture, so take the time to greet people with a handshake or a polite "Good morning" or "Good afternoon."
- **Dress Modestly**: Zambia is a relatively conservative country. It's advisable to dress modestly, especially when visiting villages, religious sites, or rural areas.
- **Respect for Elders**: Respect for elders is a cornerstone of Zambian culture. It's customary to greet elders first and offer them the best seats during gatherings.
- **Electricity and Plug Type**
  Zambia uses the **British-style three-pin plug (Type G)** and operates on a **230V, 50Hz** electrical system. If your devices use a

different plug type, make sure to bring a suitable adapter or converter.

Communication and Internet

- **SIM Cards**: Local SIM cards are widely available at airports, stores, and kiosks. The main mobile network providers are MTN, Airtel, and Zamtel. Having a local SIM can be cheaper for data and calls.
- **Internet Access**: Internet is available in most hotels, restaurants, and cafes in urban areas, but it can be slower in remote locations. It's advisable to purchase a local data plan if you need constant internet access.
- **Time Zone**
Zambia is in the **Central Africa Time Zone (CAT)**, which is **UTC +2**. There is no daylight saving time, so the time remains consistent throughout the year.

Best Time to Visit Zambia

The best time to visit Zambia for safaris and wildlife viewing is during the **dry season** from **May to October**. This is when animals congregate around water sources, making them easier to spot.

The **rainy season** (November to April) is ideal for birdwatching and enjoying Zambia's lush landscapes, though some areas may be inaccessible due to flooded roads.

By following these tips, first-time visitors to Zambia will be well-prepared to navigate the country with ease, ensuring a safe and enriching travel experience.

CHAPTER TWO

Top Attractions and Must-Visit Destinations

Victoria Falls

Victoria Falls, locally known as **Mosi-oa-Tunya** (The Smoke That Thunders), is one of the most awe-inspiring natural wonders in the world.

Straddling the border between **Zambia** and **Zimbabwe**, the falls are a UNESCO World Heritage site and one of the **Seven Natural Wonders of the World**. With a width of over 1,700 meters (5,600 feet) and a height of 108 meters (354 feet), it is considered the largest waterfall in the world by width and the largest sheet of falling water on the planet.

Key Features of Victoria Falls:

The Falls
The sheer scale of Victoria Falls is breathtaking. The Zambezi River cascades down the cliff, creating a massive spray of mist that can be seen from miles away, particularly during the rainy season when the falls are at their most powerful. The constant roar of the water gives the falls their name, "The Smoke That Thunders."

Viewing Points
Victoria Falls is accessible from both **Livingstone** in Zambia and **Victoria Falls Town** in Zimbabwe, with each side offering different viewpoints:

- **Zambian Side**: Offers a more intimate experience, with viewpoints that bring you closer to the falls. The **Knife-Edge Bridge** provides an excellent view of the main

waterfall and the Boiling Pot, where the river churns before turning downstream.
- **Zimbabwean Side**: Known for its panoramic views, this side offers a wide-angle perspective of the falls and is often considered the best for taking in the full spectacle. The **Victoria Falls Rainforest** offers various viewpoints along the trail.
- **The Devil's Pool**
One of the most thrilling experiences at Victoria Falls is the opportunity to swim in the **Devil's Pool**, a natural infinity pool right at the edge of the falls. This can be done during the dry season (usually from **September to December**), when the water levels are low enough to allow for safe swimming. A guided tour takes you to the pool, where you can swim and peer over the edge of the falls into the gorge below.

Activities Around Victoria Falls

Victoria Falls is not only about viewing the falls but also offers a wide range of activities for adventure seekers:

- **Bungee Jumping**: Jump from the **Victoria Falls Bridge** (111 meters) over the Zambezi River, one of the highest bungee jumping points in the world.

- **White-Water Rafting**: The Zambezi River offers some of the world's most exciting white-water rafting experiences, with rapids ranging from class III to V.
- **Helicopter Flights**: A helicopter ride offers a bird's-eye view of Victoria Falls, providing a spectacular perspective of the falls and the surrounding landscape.
- **Walking Safari**: Take a walking safari along the falls to spot wildlife, such as monkeys, baboons, and a variety of birds, while learning about the local ecology.
- **Sunset Cruises**: A relaxing boat trip on the Zambezi River, especially in the late afternoon, offers stunning views of the falls and opportunities to see wildlife.

Victoria Falls Bridge

The **Victoria Falls Bridge**, which spans the Zambezi River, is an iconic structure linking **Zambia** and **Zimbabwe**. The bridge itself is a historic landmark and a gateway for visitors traveling between the two countries. It offers excellent views of the falls and is a popular spot for bungee jumping and bridge walking.

Best Time to Visit

- **High Water (February to May)**: During this time, the falls are in full flow, and the volume of water cascading over the cliff is at its peak, creating the most dramatic display of mist and thunderous noise.
- **Low Water (June to September)**: Ideal for those wanting to swim in **Devil's Pool** or experience better visibility. The reduced water flow also makes it easier to walk along the river's edge and explore the surrounding area.
- **Dry Season (October to December)**: The water levels are lower, but the falls still offer an impressive spectacle. This is the best time for certain activities like swimming in Devil's Pool and exploring the falls from Zambia.

Visiting Victoria Falls

Victoria Falls is easily accessible, with flights from **Lusaka** (Zambia) and **Harare** (Zimbabwe) to **Livingstone** and **Victoria Falls Town**. From there, taxis, buses, and private vehicles can take you to the falls. Visitors can also access both the Zambian and Zimbabwean sides, though it's essential to check visa requirements and border crossing regulations before traveling.

Victoria Falls is a must-see destination for anyone visiting Zambia or Zimbabwe. Whether you are marveling at its immense power from a viewing point, getting a closer look with a helicopter tour, or engaging in adrenaline-pumping activities like bungee jumping, Victoria Falls promises an unforgettable experience.

South Luangwa & Kafue National Parks

Zambia is renowned for its exceptional wildlife and pristine natural landscapes, with two of the country's most famous national parks—**South Luangwa National Park** and **Kafue National Park**—offering some of the best safari experiences in Africa. These parks are perfect for nature lovers, wildlife enthusiasts, and adventure seekers looking to explore Zambia's rich biodiversity.

South Luangwa National Park

South Luangwa National Park is one of the most celebrated wildlife destinations in Africa, known for its exceptional game viewing and unique walking safaris. Located in the eastern part of Zambia, along the banks of the **Luangwa River**, this park is home to a wide variety of animals, including the "Big Five" (lion, elephant, buffalo, leopard, and rhino) as well as a rich diversity of bird species.

Key Features:

Diverse Wildlife

South Luangwa is a wildlife paradise, offering some of the best opportunities to see wildlife in their natural habitat. Key species include:

- **Leopards**: South Luangwa is considered one of the best places in Africa to spot leopards, especially at dawn or dusk when these elusive predators are most active.
- **Elephants and Buffalo**: The park is home to large herds of elephants and buffalo, which are frequently seen grazing along the riverbanks.
- **Hippos and Crocodiles**: The Luangwa River attracts large numbers of hippos and crocodiles, providing an excellent

opportunity for river-based wildlife viewing.
- **Wild Dogs**: The endangered African wild dog can also be spotted in the park, particularly around the remote areas of the park.

Walking Safaris

South Luangwa is one of the few places in Africa where visitors can take **walking safaris**, offering a more immersive experience in the wilderness. Guided by experienced rangers, these walking safaris allow you to see the bush up close and learn about the smaller creatures, tracks, and plants that make up the ecosystem.

Birdwatching

With over 400 species of birds, South Luangwa is a haven for birdwatchers. Expect to see a variety of waterfowl, raptors, and colorful species like the lilac-breasted roller and the African fish eagle.

Best Time to Visit

The dry season from **May to October** is ideal for game viewing, as animals congregate around water sources, making them easier to spot. The wet season (November to April) offers lush scenery and excellent birdwatching opportunities, though some areas may be less accessible due to flooding.

Accommodation

South Luangwa offers a range of accommodation options, from luxury lodges to budget-friendly campsites. Many of the lodges provide guided safaris and walking tours. Notable options include **The Luangwa River Lodge**, **Kuyenda Camp**, and **Nsefu Camp**.

Kafue National Park

Kafue National Park is Zambia's largest and oldest national park, covering an area of over **22,000**

square kilometers. Located in the western part of Zambia, Kafue is a haven for wildlife and is known for its stunning landscapes, diverse ecosystems, and abundant game. The park's vastness and remote location mean that visitors can often experience a sense of solitude and tranquility, with far fewer crowds compared to other African safari destinations.

Key Features:

Vast Ecosystems and Scenic Beauty

Kafue is home to a range of different landscapes, from **mopane woodlands** and **savannas** to **wetlands** and **riverine forests**. The park is intersected by the **Kafue River**, which provides essential water sources for wildlife, especially during the dry season. The diversity of habitats ensures a high level of biodiversity, making it a prime location for safaris.

Wildlife

Kafue National Park is home to an incredible variety of animals, including:

- **Big Cats**: Lions, leopards, and cheetahs are commonly spotted in Kafue, along with numerous smaller predators like hyenas and jackals.

- **Elephants and Buffalo**: Large herds of elephants and buffalo roam the park, often near the river and in the park's central regions.
- **Zebra and Giraffe**: Kafue is also known for its large populations of plains game, such as zebra, giraffe, impala, and wildebeest.
- **Birdlife**: The park is an excellent location for birdwatching, with over 500 species, including the **African fish eagle**, **marabou stork**, and **saddle-billed stork**.

Water-Based Activities

Kafue offers **boat safaris** along the Kafue River, providing a unique opportunity to observe wildlife from a different perspective. These safaris offer great chances to see hippos, crocodiles, and various bird species along the water's edge.

Best Time to Visit

The best time to visit Kafue is during the dry season, from **June to October**, when animals are concentrated around waterholes, making it easier to spot them. The wet season (November to April) brings lush greenery and an increase in wildlife activity, especially birdlife.

Accommodation

Kafue has a variety of lodges and camps, ranging

from rustic bush camps to more luxurious options. Some popular accommodations include **Musekese Camp**, **Shumba Camp**, and **Ila Safari Lodge**. Most lodges offer both game drives and walking safaris to explore the park.

Comparing South Luangwa & Kafue

Both **South Luangwa** and **Kafue National Parks** offer unique safari experiences, but each has its distinctive appeal:

- **South Luangwa** is renowned for its walking safaris and its reputation as one of the best places to see leopards and other wildlife up close.
- **Kafue** offers a larger, less visited experience, with more diverse landscapes and greater opportunities for water-based safaris.

Whether you're looking for a more intimate, guided safari experience in South Luangwa or seeking the vast, remote beauty of Kafue, both parks are exceptional choices for an unforgettable African adventure.

Livingstone and Lusaka

Zambia's two key cities, **Livingstone** and **Lusaka**, offer contrasting yet complementary experiences for visitors. Livingstone is the gateway to the world-famous **Victoria Falls**, while Lusaka, the capital city, is the country's economic and cultural hub. Both cities are essential stops on any Zambian itinerary, providing opportunities to explore Zambia's history, culture, and natural wonders.

Livingstone

Located in the southern part of Zambia, **Livingstone** is a small but vibrant city best known as the home of **Victoria Falls**, one of the Seven Natural Wonders of the World. The city has a laid-back charm and is a popular destination for tourists visiting the falls and surrounding attractions.

Key Features:

Victoria Falls

Livingstone is the Zambian side's closest city to **Victoria Falls**, one of the most spectacular waterfalls in the world. Visitors can enjoy a range of activities, from guided tours of the falls to adventurous experiences like **bungee jumping** off the Victoria Falls Bridge, **white-water rafting** on the Zambezi River, and helicopter flights over the falls.

Livingstone Museum:

The museum showcases Zambia's history, from ancient civilizations to colonial times and independence. It also has exhibits dedicated to the exploration of Africa and the life of **David Livingstone**, the Scottish missionary and explorer who first documented the falls.

Adventurous Activities

- **Zambezi River Cruises**: Relax on a sunset cruise along the Zambezi River, where you can spot wildlife like elephants, hippos, and crocodiles while enjoying the stunning sunset.
- **Devil's Pool**: One of the most thrilling experiences at Victoria Falls is swimming in the **Devil's Pool**, a natural rock pool right at the edge of the falls. It's a must-do during the dry season when the water levels are low enough to allow safe access.

Mosi-oa-Tunya National Park

This park, named after Victoria Falls (Mosi-oa-Tunya), is located near Livingstone and offers the chance to spot game like elephants, giraffes, and zebras, as well as birdwatching opportunities. Walking safaris are also available for those wanting a more immersive experience.

Best Time to Visit

The best time to visit Livingstone is during the dry season from **May to October** for the best views of Victoria Falls. However, the wet season (November to April) offers lush greenery and good birdwatching opportunities.

Accommodation

Livingstone has a variety of accommodation options ranging from luxury lodges to more affordable guesthouses. Popular options include **The Royal Livingstone Hotel**, **Tongabezi Lodge**, and **Zambezi Waterfront Lodge**.

Lusaka

Lusaka, the capital city of Zambia, is the country's largest and most cosmopolitan city. Located in the central part of Zambia, Lusaka is the economic, political, and cultural heart of the nation. Though it may not have the natural beauty of Livingstone,

Lusaka is a bustling city that offers a blend of modern amenities, local culture, and vibrant markets.

Key Features:

Cultural and Historical Attractions

- **National Museum**: Lusaka's National Museum is a great place to learn about Zambia's cultural and historical heritage. It has exhibits on Zambian art, archaeology, and traditional crafts.
- **Freedom Statue**: Located in the city center, the **Freedom Statue** commemorates Zambia's independence from British colonial rule in 1964 and is an iconic landmark of Lusaka.
- **The Kabwata Cultural Village**: This village offers visitors the chance to explore traditional Zambian crafts, music, and dance. Local artisans showcase wood carvings, beadwork, and fabrics, making it an excellent place for cultural souvenirs.
- **Vibrant Markets**
Lusaka is famous for its lively markets, where you can buy local crafts, fresh produce, and clothing. Key markets include:

- **The Soweto Market**: A bustling market where you can experience the local Zambian way of life. It's an excellent place to buy fresh fruit, vegetables, and Zambian spices.
- **The Craft Market**: Located near the city center, the Craft Market is a great place to buy handmade items like traditional masks, woven baskets, and beaded jewelry.
- **Parks and Green Spaces**
  Lusaka is a green city, with several parks and nature reserves within or near the city limits:
- **Lilayi Elephant Nursery**: This sanctuary is located just outside Lusaka and provides an opportunity to see orphaned elephants being rehabilitated.
- **Munda Wanga Environmental Park**: This park features a zoo, botanical gardens, and nature trails, offering a peaceful escape from the city.

Dining and Nightlife

Lusaka has a thriving restaurant scene, offering everything from traditional Zambian dishes to international cuisine. Popular restaurants include **The Royal Palm Restaurant**, **The Lusaka Grill,** and **Café Zambezi**. Lusaka also has a growing nightlife scene, with bars, clubs, and live music venues. For a taste of Zambian music, visit **The Loft** or **Jolly Boys Bar** for a night of local tunes and dancing.

Best Time to Visit

Lusaka is a year-round destination, with warm weather throughout the year. The best time to visit is during the **dry season** from **May to October**, when the weather is cooler and the city is more vibrant with events and activities.

Accommodation

Lusaka has a wide range of accommodations, from budget options to luxury hotels. Popular places to stay include the **InterContinental Lusaka**, **Radisson Blu Lusaka**, and **The Edge Boutique Hotel**.

Comparing Livingstone & Lusaka

- **Livingstone**: A small, tourist-focused city best known for its proximity to **Victoria Falls**. It's ideal for those looking to explore natural wonders, engage in adventurous activities, and enjoy a more relaxed atmosphere.
- **Lusaka**: Zambia's bustling capital, perfect for those interested in culture, shopping,

dining, and exploring the country's economic and political heart. It offers a more urban experience compared to Livingstone.

While **Livingstone** is primarily a gateway for tourists seeking outdoor adventure and natural beauty, **Lusaka** provides a deeper cultural immersion and a glimpse into modern Zambian life. Both cities are vital parts of any Zambian travel experience, offering different yet equally enriching perspectives on this diverse country.

Off-the-Beaten-Path Destinations

Zambia is famous for its major attractions like **Victoria Falls** and **South Luangwa National Park**, but the country is also home to a host of hidden gems that are less crowded and offer a more authentic and unique experience. If you're looking to explore beyond the usual tourist spots, here are some **off-the-beaten-path destinations** in Zambia that promise unforgettable adventures:

1. Lower Zambezi National Park

Located on the southern banks of the **Zambezi River, Lower Zambezi National Park** is a stunning, relatively unexplored wilderness. It offers a mix of riverine and woodland ecosystems and is known for its exceptional wildlife, including lions, elephants, hippos, and wild dogs. The park is smaller and less visited than some of Zambia's other national parks, providing an intimate safari experience.

Highlights:

- **Boat Safaris**: Explore the Zambezi River by boat, where you can see wildlife along the riverbanks, including large herds of elephants.
- **Canoeing Safaris**: For the more adventurous, canoe safaris provide an up-close view of the river and its wildlife, including hippos and crocodiles.
- **Fishing**: The Zambezi is famous for tiger fishing, which attracts anglers from around the world.

Best Time to Visit: Dry season (May to October)

2. Liuwa Plain National Park

One of Zambia's most remote and least visited national parks, **Liuwa Plain National Park** is an untouched sanctuary for wildlife enthusiasts seeking solitude and adventure. Situated in the western part of Zambia, the park is known for its vast, flat plains, seasonal floods, and impressive wildlife migrations.

Highlights:

- **Wildlife Migration**: Liuwa is one of the few places in Africa where visitors can witness a wildebeest migration, comparable to that of the Serengeti.
- **Lion Population**: The park has a small but growing population of lions, which are often seen hunting during the dry season.
- **Birdwatching**: With over 300 bird species, Liuwa is a haven for birdwatchers, especially during the wet season when migratory birds arrive.

Best Time to Visit: Dry season (May to October), though the wet season offers a unique birdwatching experience.

3. Nsumbu National Park

Located on the shores of **Lake Tanganyika** in the northern part of Zambia, **Nsumbu National Park** is one of the country's most remote and least explored destinations. The park is a tropical paradise with lush forests, beautiful beaches, and clear waters, making it a perfect spot for those looking to combine wildlife and water-based activities.

Highlights:

- **Lake Tanganyika**: The crystal-clear waters of the lake provide excellent opportunities for swimming, snorkeling, and fishing.
- **Chioya Bay**: This picturesque bay is ideal for peaceful relaxation and exploring the surrounding forests and beaches.
- **Wildlife Viewing**: The park is home to elephants, buffalo, leopards, and a variety of antelope, along with an array of bird species.

Best Time to Visit: Dry season (May to October)

4. Kalambo Falls

For those looking to experience the beauty of **Zambia's waterfalls** without the crowds, **Kalambo Falls** is a hidden gem. Located in the far north of Zambia, near the Tanzanian border, Kalambo Falls is one of the tallest waterfalls in Africa, with a drop of around 221 meters (725 feet). The falls are situated in a remote area, making it a great destination for those seeking tranquility and natural beauty.

Highlights:

- **Hiking**: The journey to Kalambo Falls is a rewarding experience, with scenic views of the surrounding forest and cliffs.
- **Cultural Heritage**: The area around the falls is home to **archaeological sites** where ancient stone tools have been discovered, adding historical significance to the area.

Best Time to Visit: Dry season (May to October)

5. The Bangweulu Wetlands

The **Bangweulu Wetlands** in northern Zambia are a vast and remote network of swamps, lakes, and floodplains. The wetlands are a paradise for birdwatchers, with over 400 species of birds, including the rare **black-cheeked lovebird**. This area is relatively untouched by tourism, making it perfect for those looking for an off-the-grid experience.

Highlights:

- **Birdwatching**: The wetlands are home to a diverse range of birdlife, including endangered species such as the **African finfoot** and **pelicans**.
- **Fishing and Boat Tours**: Explore the wetlands by boat and enjoy fishing and spotting wildlife, including elephants, crocodiles, and hippos.
- **Cultural Experience**: The nearby **Chishinga people** offer visitors the chance to experience local traditions and crafts.

Best Time to Visit: Dry season (May to October)

6. Kafue River and Its Surroundings

The **Kafue River** flows through **Kafue National Park** and is a vital lifeline for much of Zambia's wildlife. However, it is also an ideal location for exploring remote areas and pristine nature. The river and surrounding region offer opportunities for canoeing, fishing, and wildlife viewing in a much quieter setting than the more famous parks.

Highlights:

- **Kafue River Cruises**: Explore the river by boat, where you can enjoy peaceful

surroundings and see hippos, crocodiles, and birdlife.
- **Fishing**: The river is renowned for its **tiger fish**, making it a popular spot for anglers.
- **Remote Camping**: For the ultimate off-the-beaten-path experience, camp along the river in remote, wild locations.

Best Time to Visit: Dry season (May to October)

7. Remote Villages in Northern Zambia

Zambia's remote villages offer a glimpse into traditional life that has remained largely unchanged for centuries. Visiting villages in areas like **Muchinga Province** or **Northern Province** can provide a unique cultural experience, with opportunities to engage with local tribes and learn about traditional customs, food, and crafts.

Highlights:

- **Traditional Ceremonies**: Depending on when you visit, you may be able to witness local ceremonies and festivals that are integral to the culture of Zambian tribes, such as the **Nc'wala Ceremony** of the Ngoni people.

- **Crafts and Arts**: Many villages offer handmade crafts, such as baskets, beads, and wooden carvings, that reflect the rich cultural heritage of Zambia.
- **Eco-Tourism**: Some villages have adopted eco-tourism initiatives, offering homestays, guided tours, and opportunities to participate in local farming and fishing activities.

Best Time to Visit: Dry season (May to October)

Zambia's off-the-beaten-path destinations offer a wealth of opportunities for those seeking adventure, tranquility, and cultural immersion. Whether you're hiking to remote waterfalls, exploring wetlands teeming with wildlife, or discovering hidden wildlife sanctuaries, these destinations provide a more intimate experience with Zambia's stunning natural beauty and rich cultural heritage. For those who venture off the well-trodden paths, Zambia offers an abundance of rewards.

Unique Experiences and Hidden Gems

Zambia is a country full of surprises, offering a wealth of **unique experiences** and **hidden gems** that are often overlooked by traditional tourists. From remote wilderness areas and cultural adventures to thrilling activities in breathtaking locations, Zambia provides unforgettable moments for those who venture off the beaten path. Here are some of the country's most unique experiences and hidden gems:

1. Walking Safaris in South Luangwa National Park

While safaris in Zambia are known for their wildlife viewing, the **walking safari** in **South Luangwa National Park** offers an entirely different, more immersive experience. Guided by expert local guides, walking safaris provide the chance to learn about the ecosystem up close, from tracking animals to identifying plants and smaller creatures often missed on traditional game drives.

Why It's Unique:

- South Luangwa is one of the few places in the world where you can embark on walking safaris in a safe and guided environment.
- Experience the thrill of coming face to face with nature as you explore the park's diverse landscapes on foot.

2. Devil's Pool at Victoria Falls

Devil's Pool is one of the most exhilarating natural pools in the world, located right on the edge of **Victoria Falls**. During the dry season, visitors can swim in the pool, which sits just inches from the mighty falls, offering a thrilling and jaw-dropping experience.

Why It's Unique:

- Swimming in Devil's Pool is an unparalleled experience where you can look over the edge of one of the world's most famous waterfalls.
- Only accessible during the dry season, this experience is a must for adventurous travelers.

3. Kafue River Canoeing

Canoeing along the **Kafue River** in Zambia's **Kafue National Park** offers a peaceful, yet exhilarating, way to experience the country's wildlife. As you paddle along the river, you'll glide past hippos, crocodiles, and a variety of bird species, all from a unique perspective.

Why It's Unique:

- A canoeing safari offers an intimate connection to nature, allowing you to observe wildlife from the river's edge.
- The stillness of the water makes for an incredibly peaceful experience, ideal for nature lovers and those seeking quiet reflection.

4. Liuwa Plain National Park and the Wildebeest Migration

One of Zambia's best-kept secrets is **Liuwa Plain National Park**, which offers a rare and remote safari experience. The park is home to one of Africa's least known but most extraordinary wildlife migrations: the **wildebeest migration**.

Unlike the famous Serengeti migration, Liuwa offers a quieter, more intimate experience, allowing visitors to witness this incredible natural event in solitude.

Why It's Unique:

- **Liuwa Plain** offers one of Africa's most untouched and authentic wildlife experiences, with a fraction of the visitors compared to more famous parks.
- The park is one of the few places in Africa where you can witness a wildebeest migration, making it a unique destination for safari enthusiasts.

5. The Chobe River Cruise

While the **Chobe River** is often associated with **Botswana**, the Zambian section of the river offers a less-crowded, unique experience. A river cruise along the **Chobe River** provides opportunities to see elephants, hippos, and crocodiles, as well as stunning views of the surrounding wilderness.

Why It's Unique:

- The Zambian section of the river is less commercialized than the Botswanan side,

providing a more peaceful and private experience.
- The river's proximity to **Victoria Falls** and **Chobe National Park** means you can enjoy both wildlife viewing and beautiful scenery.

6. The Remote Village of Kazungula

Kazungula is a remote village located at the intersection of **Zambia**, **Botswana**, **Zimbabwe**, and **Namibia**. This small but culturally rich village offers a unique glimpse into the traditional lifestyles of Zambia's people. You can visit the village, meet the locals, and experience the rural Zambian way of life, far from the typical tourist routes.

Why It's Unique:

- Experience authentic Zambian village life, including local markets, traditional dances, and community events.
- The village is located near the **Kazungula Ferry**, where four countries meet, adding an intriguing cross-border element to your visit.

7. Remote Hiking in the Muchinga Mountains

For the adventurous traveler, the **Muchinga Mountains** in northern Zambia offer some of the best hiking opportunities in the country. This remote area, which runs parallel to the **Great Rift Valley**, features breathtaking views, lush forests, and diverse wildlife. The hiking trails are less known, allowing for a peaceful trek through Zambia's untamed wilderness.

Why It's Unique:

- A truly off-the-beaten-path destination, the Muchinga Mountains provide a rare opportunity to explore rugged terrain in solitude.
- Along the hike, you'll pass through traditional villages, pristine forests, and valleys, with the occasional sighting of animals like monkeys and antelopes.

8. The Bangweulu Wetlands and the Shoebill Stork

For birdwatchers, the **Bangweulu Wetlands** are one of the most unique and lesser-known ecosystems in Zambia. The wetlands are home to a variety of bird species, including the rare **shoebill stork**, which is a major draw for ornithologists and photographers.

Why It's Unique:

- The wetlands offer some of the best birdwatching in Zambia, including the chance to see the **shoebill**, one of the world's most elusive and prehistoric-looking birds.
- The region's remote location provides a peaceful, undisturbed environment to observe wildlife in its natural habitat.

9. The Hidden Caves of Kafue Gorge

The **Kafue Gorge** near **Kafue River** is home to a series of **hidden caves**, some of which are only accessible by local guides. These caves are steeped in history and offer a fascinating experience for those interested in Zambia's geology and ancient history.

Why It's Unique:

- The Kafue Gorge caves are relatively unexplored, providing a sense of adventure and discovery.
- Some caves contain prehistoric rock art, offering insight into the region's ancient human history.

10. Traditional Copperbelt Mining Tours

The **Copperbelt region** in Zambia is known for its rich mining history, and visitors can take unique tours to explore the industrial heritage of the area. These tours offer a glimpse into Zambia's copper mining legacy, showcasing how the industry has shaped the country's economy and culture.

Why It's Unique:

- Learn about Zambia's **mining heritage** and the historical significance of the **Copperbelt** in a way that few tourists experience.
- The tours often include visits to old mining towns, factories, and local communities, providing a deeper understanding of Zambia's industrial past.

Zambia offers a wealth of **unique experiences** and **hidden gems** that allow travelers to explore the country's natural beauty, culture, and history in exciting and often off-the-beaten-path ways. Whether you're swimming in Devil's Pool, hiking the Muchinga Mountains, or witnessing a rare wildlife migration in Liuwa Plain, these experiences are perfect for those seeking adventure and authenticity. Zambia is a land of surprises, waiting for the curious traveler to uncover its many treasures.

CHAPTER THREE

Zambian Cuisine and Dining

Traditional Zambian Dishes

Zambian cuisine reflects the country's rich cultural diversity and natural resources, offering a variety of delicious and hearty dishes. Traditional meals are often based on staples like **maize**, **cassava**, and **millet**, complemented by fresh vegetables, meats, and fish. Here are some of the most beloved and traditional Zambian dishes:

1. Nshima (Sadza)

The cornerstone of Zambian cuisine, **Nshima** is a simple yet filling dish made from ground maize (corn) flour. It is typically served as a starchy accompaniment to meat, fish, or vegetables. Nshima is similar to **sadza** (Zimbabwe), **ugali** (Kenya), or **posho** (Uganda) and is eaten by hand, often rolled into a ball and dipped into sauces.

Why It's Special:

- Nshima is a **daily staple** in most Zambian households.
- It is served with a variety of sides such as vegetables, stews, or grilled meat, making it a versatile dish.

2. Ifishimu (Fish)

Given Zambia's abundant water bodies, fish is an important part of the diet. **Ifishimu** typically refers to **freshwater fish**, like **bream** or **tilapia**, that are fried, grilled, or cooked in a tomato-based sauce. **Bream** from **Lake Tanganyika** and **Lake Kariba** is particularly prized.

Why It's Special:

- Fish is often prepared with **tomatoes, onions, garlic**, and sometimes a bit of chili for flavor.
- It's a healthy and popular choice, especially for those living near lakes or rivers.

3. Chikanda (African Polony)

Sometimes called **African polony** or **wild vegetable sausage**, **Chikanda** is a unique dish made from the tuber of the **orchid plant**. The tuber is grated, mixed with peanuts, and then cooked into a savory cake-like dish. It's often served alongside nshima or other dishes.

Why It's Special:

- **Chikanda** is a traditional delicacy that highlights Zambia's unique plant-based foods.
- It's rich in protein and widely consumed in the **Eastern and Southern regions** of Zambia.

4. Ubwabwa (Cassava)

Cassava, known locally as **Ibwabwa**, is another staple in the Zambian diet, especially in the **northern regions**. It's a root vegetable that can be boiled, fried, or pounded into a flour, which is then used to make a kind of dough or paste. The flavor is neutral, making it a perfect side dish to complement spicy stews and meat.

Why It's Special:

- Cassava is an important **carbohydrate source**, particularly in regions where maize is less abundant.
- It is often served with fish or vegetable stews, providing a hearty meal.

5. Mungongo (Groundnut Stew)

Mungongo is a **groundnut (peanut) stew**, typically made with peanuts, tomatoes, onions, and chili peppers. It is a rich and savory dish often served with nshima or rice, and it may include vegetables like spinach, okra, or pumpkin leaves.

Why It's Special:

- **Groundnuts** are a popular crop in Zambia, and this dish makes use of their creamy, nutty flavor.
- It is often prepared as a vegetarian option but can also be enhanced with chicken or beef.

6. Chibwantu (Fermented Millet Drink)

Chibwana is a traditional **fermented drink** made from millet, maize, or sorghum. It has a slightly sour taste due to fermentation and is usually served chilled. It is enjoyed by Zambians during ceremonies, festivals, and other communal events.

Why It's Special:

- **Chibwantu** is a part of Zambia's **cultural identity**, often made at home in villages.
- It's refreshing and acts as a natural probiotic due to the fermentation process.

7. Imambara (Zambian Stew)

Imambara is a hearty, traditional stew made from a combination of beef, chicken, or fish, and often includes vegetables like **pumpkin leaves** (chibwabwa), **spinach**, and **tomatoes**. This stew is usually served alongside nshima and offers a rich, flavorful meal.

Why It's Special:

- It's a perfect blend of protein, fiber, and vegetables, making it both nutritious and filling.
- The use of local herbs and spices gives it a distinct Zambian flavor.

8. Kapenta (Small Fish)

Kapenta, also known as **lake sardines**, are tiny fish typically found in **Lake Tanganyika** and **Lake Kariba**. They are sun-dried and then fried or cooked in a tomato sauce. Kapenta is often served with nshima and vegetables, making it a favorite meal in many Zambian households.

Why It's Special:

- Kapenta is rich in **omega-3 fatty acids** and is an affordable source of protein.
- It is an essential part of the diet for people living near Zambia's lakes.

9. Tute (Sweet Potatoes)

In Zambia, **sweet potatoes (Tute)** are a popular side dish, often boiled or roasted and served with a variety of stews. They are commonly paired with dishes like **Chikanda**, **Kapenta**, or **Mungongo** for a balanced meal.

Why It's Special:

- **Sweet potatoes** are highly nutritious and are a source of **vitamins A and C**.
- They are a versatile food that complements both meat and vegetable dishes.

10. Masala Chips

A fusion dish with Indian influences, **Masala Chips** is a popular street food in Zambia. It consists of

French fries (chips) fried with onions, tomatoes, and a blend of spices such as curry powder, turmeric, and chili. It is often eaten as a snack or served as a side dish to complement grilled meats or stews.

Why It's Special:

- It combines **Indian-inspired flavors** with a locally loved comfort food—potatoes.
- Masala Chips is a quick and satisfying meal, loved by locals and visitors alike.

Traditional Zambian dishes offer a flavorful journey through the country's culture and heritage. From the staple **nshima** to the deliciously unique **chikanda** and **mungongo**, these meals reflect the diversity of Zambia's ethnic groups, natural resources, and culinary traditions. Exploring Zambian cuisine is an essential part of any visit to the country, as it offers a window into the heart of its culture and the daily lives of its people.

Recommended Restaurants and Local Dining Spots

Zambia offers a wide variety of dining options, from casual street food stalls to fine dining establishments that showcase the rich flavors of the country's traditional cuisine and international dishes. Whether you're craving authentic Zambian dishes or a more contemporary culinary experience, here are some of the best restaurants and local dining spots to explore during your visit.

1. The Tasting Room, Lusaka

Located in **Lusaka**, Zambia's capital, **The Tasting Room** offers a fine dining experience that blends **local Zambian ingredients** with international culinary techniques. The restaurant is known for its elegant ambiance, exceptional service, and unique tasting menus, which feature both meat and vegetarian options. The wine list is extensive, and the restaurant's farm-to-table approach emphasizes fresh, local produce.

Why It's Recommended:

- **Innovative dining experience** combining local and global flavors.
- Ideal for a **special occasion** or an upscale dining experience.

2. The Boma – Place of BBQ, Livingstone

Located near the famous **Victoria Falls**, **The Boma** is a popular spot for both locals and tourists looking to enjoy a traditional Zambian feast. This vibrant restaurant offers a lively atmosphere where guests can enjoy a **buffet-style meal** with a wide range of Zambian delicacies, including **nyama choma** (grilled meat), **nshima**, and **Kapenta**. You can also sample game meats like **warthog** and **kudu**. The Boma provides live traditional music and dancing, making it a fun, cultural dining experience.

Why It's Recommended:

- Offers **authentic Zambian cuisine** and cultural entertainment.

- Perfect for those visiting **Victoria Falls** and seeking a memorable dining experience.

3. Cafe Zambezi, Lusaka

Located in **Lusaka**, **Cafe Zambezi** is a relaxed and trendy restaurant serving **Zambian and African-inspired cuisine**. The menu features a mix of dishes, from hearty stews to lighter fare, as well as a selection of seafood and meats. The outdoor terrace and chic interior make it a great spot for lunch or dinner. Their **signature Zambezi burger** and a wide variety of cocktails are crowd favorites.

Why It's Recommended:

- A **casual yet stylish** atmosphere perfect for an afternoon meal or dinner.
- Known for **local specialties** like bream and zambian-style curries.

4. Marlin Restaurant, Livingstone

Located just a short distance from **Victoria Falls**, **Marlin Restaurant** offers a delicious selection of international dishes with an emphasis on fresh seafood. The restaurant's relaxed ambiance, paired with its extensive menu, makes it a great place for both lunch and dinner. The signature dishes include **fish and chips**, **grilled prawns**, and **mushroom steaks**.

Why It's Recommended:

- Known for its **fresh seafood** and European-style dishes.
- Offers a great place to unwind after a visit to **Victoria Falls**.

5. 7 Nandi, Lusaka

If you're in **Lusaka** and craving some of the best Zambian street food, **7 Nandi** is the place to be. This casual eatery specializes in **nyama choma (grilled meat)** served with nshima, vegetables, and various traditional side dishes. It's a popular spot for both locals and tourists who want to experience the authentic taste of **Zambian barbecue**.

Why It's Recommended:

- Great for an **authentic Zambian street food experience**.

- **Casual and vibrant** atmosphere perfect for a relaxed meal.

6. The Royal Restaurant, Lusaka

For those seeking a more **luxurious dining experience**, **The Royal Restaurant** in **Lusaka** offers an elegant setting with a mix of **Zambian and Chinese cuisines**. The menu features a selection of local dishes as well as Chinese-inspired offerings, and their extensive menu ensures there's something for everyone. Known for its quality ingredients and exceptional service, this restaurant is perfect for a special dinner.

Why It's Recommended:

- A fusion of **Zambian and Chinese cuisines**, offering variety.
- Excellent for a **fine dining experience** in Lusaka.

7. Zambezi Restaurant, Livingstone

Located in the heart of **Livingstone**, the **Zambezi Restaurant** provides a scenic dining experience overlooking the Zambezi River. Guests can enjoy a wide range of meals, including **Zambian staples**, **international dishes**, and a variety of drinks. The outdoor seating area is ideal for watching the sunset while enjoying delicious food, making it a romantic choice for dinner.

Why It's Recommended:

- **Scenic riverfront location**, perfect for sunset dining.
- Offers a mix of **Zambian and international dishes**.

8. The Hut, Lusaka

The Hut offers a casual but delightful dining experience with a focus on **Zambian and Southern African cuisine**. Located in **Lusaka**, this eatery serves a variety of dishes, including **stews**, **meat skewers**, and **spicy grilled chicken**. It's a great place for lunch or dinner, with a lively atmosphere that reflects the warmth of Zambian hospitality.

Why It's Recommended:

- Great for a **casual, local dining experience**.
- Known for their **grilled meats** and tasty sides.

9. Ngolide Lodge, Lusaka

Ngolide Lodge is a popular dining spot that offers both **traditional Zambian food** and **international cuisine**. The **restaurant** is set in a serene environment, ideal for a relaxed meal in Lusaka. They serve a variety of dishes, from **grilled meats** to fresh vegetables, as well as vegetarian-friendly options.

Why It's Recommended:

- Offers a **peaceful, relaxing setting** perfect for a quiet dinner.
- Known for its variety of **local and international options**.

10. The Zambezi Sun, Livingstone

The **Zambezi Sun** offers an upscale dining experience at the **Victoria Falls** area, with several restaurants and lounges offering both local and international dishes. Guests can enjoy fresh **local fish**, **game meat**, and **grilled meats**, as well as an assortment of vegetarian-friendly dishes, all set against the backdrop of lush gardens and river views.

Why It's Recommended:

- **Upscale dining** with views of the Zambezi River.
- Perfect for guests staying at the **Zambezi Sun** or those visiting **Victoria Falls**.

Zambia's restaurant scene offers something for every type of traveler, from traditional eateries serving local favorites like **nyama choma** and **nshima**, to more international offerings in upscale settings. Whether you're exploring the vibrant capital of Lusaka, the tourist-friendly Livingstone near **Victoria Falls**, or the peaceful countryside, there are plenty of spots to enjoy delicious Zambian food and experience the local hospitality.

International Cuisine Options in Zambia

While Zambia is renowned for its rich traditional dishes, the growing urbanization in cities like **Lusaka**, **Livingstone**, and **Ndola** has led to a diverse culinary scene offering international cuisine from all around the world. Whether you're craving **Italian**, **Indian**, **Chinese**, or even **Lebanese** fare, Zambia's restaurants provide a wide array of options that cater to diverse tastes. Here are some popular international cuisine options you can find in Zambia:

1. Italian Cuisine

Italian food is popular across Zambia, with many restaurants offering pizza, pasta, and other classic Italian dishes. **Wood-fired pizzas** and **fresh pasta** are common in many urban dining spots.

Notable Restaurants:

- **The Italian Kitchen** (Lusaka): Famous for its wood-fired pizzas and authentic Italian pastas, with a cozy and casual atmosphere.
- **La Toscana** (Livingstone): Known for its exquisite Italian-inspired menu, featuring a variety of pizzas, pastas, and risottos.

Dishes to Try:

- **Pizza Margherita**: A classic Italian pizza topped with mozzarella, tomatoes, and basil.
- **Pasta alla Carbonara**: Traditional pasta served with eggs, cheese, pancetta, and pepper.

2. Indian Cuisine

Indian cuisine has found a permanent place in Zambia's food culture, particularly in urban areas with a significant Indian diaspora. From flavorful curries to crispy **samosas** and **naan bread**, there are plenty of options to satisfy your cravings for aromatic spices.

Notable Restaurants:

- **The Punjab** (Lusaka): A favorite for authentic Indian dishes like butter chicken, biryani, and a variety of vegetarian curries.
- **The Royal Punjab** (Livingstone): Offers a rich variety of traditional Indian curries, tandoori items, and sweets like **gulab jamun**.

Dishes to Try:

- **Chicken Tikka Masala**: A rich and creamy curry made with marinated grilled chicken.
- **Butter Chicken**: Tender chicken cooked in a creamy tomato sauce, often paired with naan or rice.

3. Chinese Cuisine

Chinese restaurants are also quite popular in Zambia, offering everything from crispy spring rolls to flavorful **sweet and sour pork** and **fried rice**. Chinese food is a favorite for a quick and delicious meal, often served in a family-style setting.

Notable Restaurants:

- **The Golden Palace** (Lusaka): Famous for its **dim sum**, **Peking duck**, and **sweet and sour dishes**.
- **Café Zambezi** (Lusaka): A fusion of Chinese and African-inspired dishes, offering stir-fries and seafood options.

Dishes to Try:

- **Sweet and Sour Chicken**: A popular dish featuring crispy chicken tossed in a tangy sweet and sour sauce.
- **Kung Pao Chicken**: Stir-fried chicken with peanuts, vegetables, and a flavorful sauce.

4. Lebanese Cuisine

Lebanese food is becoming increasingly popular in Zambia, with many restaurants offering dishes like **hummus**, **falafel**, and **shawarma**. The combination of fresh vegetables, grilled meats, and flavorful dips makes it a great option for a light yet satisfying meal.

Notable Restaurants:

- **Mamma Mia** (Lusaka): Known for its Lebanese-inspired mezze, including **hummus**, **tabbouleh**, and **kebabs**.

- **The Lebanese Grill** (Lusaka): A cozy restaurant offering a wide range of Lebanese dishes, including **shawarma**, **kebabs**, and **baklava** for dessert.

Dishes to Try:

- **Shawarma**: A wrap or platter made with spiced meat (usually lamb or chicken) and vegetables.
- **Falafel**: Deep-fried chickpea balls served with pita bread, tahini, and fresh vegetables.

5. American Cuisine

American fast food chains are widely available in Zambia, especially in larger cities. Popular international fast food options include **burgers**, **fries**, and **fried chicken**, but there are also more refined options serving southern comfort food and steaks.

Notable Restaurants:

- **The Bronx Grill** (Lusaka): Known for its classic American-style grilled burgers, ribs, and steaks.

- **Nando's** (Various Locations): Famous for its **peri-peri chicken** with a choice of spices and sauces.

Dishes to Try:

- **Cheeseburger**: A juicy beef patty topped with cheese, lettuce, and pickles, served with fries.
- **Ribs**: Slow-cooked pork ribs slathered in barbecue sauce, often served with mashed potatoes or corn on the cob.

6. Mediterranean Cuisine

Mediterranean cuisine is another international option available in Zambia, offering lighter, fresh meals made with olive oil, vegetables, seafood, and grilled meats. These dishes are often healthy and full of flavor, making them a favorite choice.

Notable Restaurants:

- **The Mediterranean Café** (Lusaka): Offering a variety of Mediterranean-inspired dishes such as **grilled fish**, **hummus**, and **Greek salads**.
- **Spaghetti House** (Lusaka): A casual spot that serves Mediterranean and Italian

favorites, with a focus on fresh salads and grilled seafood.

Dishes to Try:

- **Grilled Fish with Lemon and Herbs**: A Mediterranean favorite, often served with grilled vegetables or couscous.
- **Greek Salad**: A refreshing salad made with cucumbers, tomatoes, olives, onions, and feta cheese.

7. French Cuisine

French cuisine is represented in Zambia through bakeries, patisseries, and fine dining restaurants. You'll find delicious pastries like **croissants** and **pain au chocolat**, along with more elaborate dishes like **coq au vin** and **ratatouille**.

Notable Restaurants:

- **Chez Pierre** (Lusaka): Known for its **French-inspired dishes** such as **duck confit**, **coq au vin**, and an excellent selection of cheeses and wines.
- **Le Parisien** (Lusaka): A French bakery and café offering a range of fresh pastries, baguettes, and light bites.

Dishes to Try:

- **Coq au Vin**: Chicken braised in wine with mushrooms, onions, and garlic.
- **Quiche Lorraine**: A savory pie filled with eggs, cream, cheese, and bacon.

8. Sushi and Japanese Cuisine

Sushi and Japanese cuisine have also found a place in Zambia, particularly in the larger cities. Restaurants offering **sushi**, **teriyaki**, and other Japanese dishes bring an exciting option for those looking for fresh, light meals.

Notable Restaurants:

- **Sushi One** (Lusaka): Offers a wide variety of **sushi rolls**, sashimi, and **teriyaki dishes**.
- **The Asian Restaurant** (Lusaka): Known for its fusion of **Japanese** and **Chinese** dishes, including **sushi** and **ramen**.

Dishes to Try:

- **California Roll**: A sushi roll made with crab, avocado, and cucumber.

- **Teriyaki Chicken**: Grilled chicken glazed with a sweet soy sauce, served with steamed rice and vegetables.

Zambia's restaurant scene offers an exciting blend of **international cuisines**, providing visitors with a variety of dining experiences beyond the traditional Zambian dishes. Whether you're in the mood for **Italian pizza**, **Indian curries**, **Chinese stir-fries**, or **Lebanese mezze**, Zambia's growing food culture has plenty of options to satisfy every craving.

CHAPTER FOUR

Accommodation and Recommended Hotels

Luxury, Mid-Range, and Budget Accommodation Options in Zambia

Zambia offers a wide range of accommodation options to suit every type of traveler, from luxurious resorts with world-class amenities to budget-friendly guesthouses that offer a comfortable and authentic experience. Whether you are looking for indulgence, comfort, or savings, here's a breakdown of the best options by price category:

Luxury Accommodation Options

For those looking for the ultimate comfort and a memorable stay, Zambia's luxury accommodations offer stunning locations, top-tier service, and world-class facilities. Many of these properties are set near iconic attractions like **Victoria Falls** and **South Luangwa National Park**, allowing guests to enjoy both luxury and adventure.

1. Royal Livingstone Hotel by Anantara, Livingstone

Located near **Victoria Falls**, this five-star hotel offers an unparalleled experience with **elegant rooms** overlooking the Zambezi River. Guests can enjoy a wide range of luxury amenities, including **fine dining**, a **spa**, and **private safaris**. The hotel provides direct access to the falls, ensuring guests have a front-row seat to one of the Seven Natural Wonders of the World.

Key Features:

- Exclusive views of **Victoria Falls**.
- Private access to the falls.
- **Infinity pool** overlooking the river.
- **Fine dining** and **spa services**.

2. Tongabezi Lodge, Livingstone

Situated on the banks of the **Zambezi River**, **Tongabezi Lodge** is a luxurious, intimate retreat offering spacious chalets, private cottages, and a treehouse for the ultimate escape. The lodge offers exclusive boat trips and guided tours to **Victoria Falls**, along with opportunities for game drives and cultural excursions.

Key Features:

- **Private boat safaris** on the Zambezi.
- **Private plunge pools** in some cottages.
- **Romantic getaway** with personal service.
- **Eco-friendly** and sustainable practices.

3. Chiawa Camp, Lower Zambezi National Park

For a truly immersive safari experience, **Chiawa Camp** offers a luxurious retreat in the heart of **Lower Zambezi National Park**. This **all-inclusive camp** offers an intimate and eco-conscious experience, with incredible game-viewing opportunities and elegant tented suites that blend seamlessly with nature.

Key Features:

- **Game drives** and **boat safaris** in Lower Zambezi.

- Spacious, stylish **tented suites** with private decks.
- Gourmet meals and **luxury bush experiences**.
- Personalized service and attention to detail.

Mid-Range Accommodation Options

For those who want comfort and convenience at a more moderate price point, Zambia has many mid-range accommodations offering quality service, good amenities, and well-located properties. These options strike a balance between affordability and luxury, ideal for families or those looking to enjoy Zambia's beauty without breaking the bank.

1. Avani Victoria Falls Resort, Livingstone

Located just a short walk from **Victoria Falls**, **Avani Victoria Falls Resort** offers great value for its prime location. The resort offers modern rooms with stunning views of the Zambezi River and access to both the falls and various activities, including guided tours, **rafting**, and **bungee jumping**.

Key Features:

- Direct access to **Victoria Falls**.
- **Family-friendly** with child care services.
- **Outdoor pool** and **fitness center**.
- On-site restaurants with diverse dining options.

2. Zambezi Sun Hotel, Livingstone

Located near the **Royal Livingstone, Zambezi Sun Hotel** provides a more affordable luxury option while still offering stunning views and excellent service. The hotel is known for its proximity to the falls and its wide range of activities such as **safari trips**, **bird watching**, and **Zambezi River cruises**.

Key Features:

- **Proximity to Victoria Falls**.
- **Swimming pool** and **spa services**.

- **African-inspired décor** with modern amenities.
- Great options for **group bookings** and **family stays**.

3. The Farmhouse, Lusaka

For those staying in the capital city, **The Farmhouse** offers a relaxing and comfortable environment, combining Zambian hospitality with modern facilities. The guesthouse features spacious rooms, a beautiful garden, and a café serving local and international dishes.

Key Features:

- **Outdoor pool** and lush gardens.
- **Eco-friendly** accommodations.
- Close to **Lusaka city center**.
- Free shuttle service from the airport.

Budget Accommodation Options

Zambia also offers a variety of budget-friendly accommodations that are perfect for backpackers, independent travelers, and those on a tighter budget. These options provide clean and comfortable rooms at an affordable price, often located in key cities or near popular attractions.

1. Jollyboys Backpackers, Livingstone

Known for its vibrant atmosphere and excellent service, **Jollyboys Backpackers** is a great option for budget travelers visiting **Victoria Falls**. The hostel offers a variety of accommodation options, from dormitory beds to private rooms, and features an on-site bar, restaurant, and pool.

Key Features:

- Affordable dorms and private rooms.
- **Social atmosphere** with organized tours and activities.
- Close proximity to **Victoria Falls** and adventure activities.

2. The Golden Leaf, Lusaka

For those staying in **Lusaka**, **The Golden Leaf** offers budget-friendly accommodation with a great location near the city center. It provides simple, clean rooms and offers a restaurant that serves traditional Zambian meals. It's a solid option for short stays or business travelers.

Key Features:

- **Affordable rates** and basic amenities.
- **Restaurant** serving Zambian dishes.
- Convenient location near the **Lusaka city center**.

3. Maramba River Lodge, Livingstone

Located on the banks of the **Maramba River**, this **budget lodge** offers affordable tented accommodations, as well as a variety of safari activities. It's a great option for those who want a mix of budget prices with the opportunity to experience Zambia's wildlife.

Key Features:

- **Tented accommodations** and chalets.
- Close to **Victoria Falls** and **game reserves**.
- Activities such as **game viewing** and **boat trips**.

Zambia offers a wide range of accommodation options, catering to every budget and preference. Whether you're looking for a **luxury resort** with stunning views of **Victoria Falls**, a **mid-range** hotel with comfortable amenities, or a **budget-friendly guesthouse** in the heart of Lusaka, you'll find a variety of choices to make your stay enjoyable.

Unique Stays in Zambia: Eco-Lodges, Camping, and Cultural Lodging

Zambia offers a variety of unique accommodation experiences that allow visitors to connect with nature and immerse themselves in the country's rich culture. From eco-lodges that emphasize sustainability to camping under the stars in Africa's wild landscapes and cultural lodges that showcase local traditions, these options provide travelers with unforgettable experiences.

1. Eco-Lodges: Sustainable Luxury Amidst Nature

Eco-lodges in Zambia offer a sustainable and immersive experience, combining luxury with environmental consciousness. These lodges are set in breathtaking natural settings and emphasize eco-friendly practices, from using solar power to supporting local conservation efforts. Staying in an eco-lodge allows you to experience Zambia's pristine environments while contributing to conservation and responsible tourism.

Notable Eco-Lodges:

Chongwe River Camp, Lower Zambezi National Park Located along the Zambezi River, **Chongwe River Camp** is an intimate eco-lodge offering an authentic safari experience. The camp emphasizes sustainability, using solar power, and its activities focus on low-impact, environmentally responsible practices such as walking safaris and canoeing.

Key Features:

- **Solar-powered** camp with eco-friendly amenities.
- Close to **Lower Zambezi National Park**, offering game drives and river safaris.
- **Sustainable tourism** practices, with a focus on wildlife conservation.

Lunga River Lodge, Kafue National Park Tucked away on the banks of the **Lunga River**, **Lunga River Lodge** is a remote eco-lodge within **Kafue National Park**. The lodge is committed to preserving the natural environment and providing guests with a low-impact, wildlife-centered experience. Guests can enjoy walking safaris, birdwatching, and exclusive game drives.

Key Features:

- **Eco-conscious** design with solar-powered systems.
- Offers **private game viewing** in a secluded area.
- Committed to preserving the natural environment and supporting the local community.

Shumba Camp, Kafue National Park Set within the **Kafue National Park**, **Shumba Camp** offers a serene escape with a focus on eco-friendly practices. The camp blends luxury with sustainability, with tented accommodations built from local materials, and activities designed to minimize the impact on the surrounding environment.

Key Features:

- **Eco-friendly** design and sustainable operations.
- **Remote location** with exclusive wildlife viewing.
- A combination of **game drives** and walking safaris.

2. Camping: A True Connection with Nature

Camping in Zambia provides an opportunity to truly immerse yourself in the country's natural beauty and wildlife. Whether you are pitching a tent at a designated campsite or opting for **luxury mobile camping**, Zambia offers a range of camping experiences, from basic sites to more comfortable, all-inclusive safari camps.

Notable Camping Options:

Luangwa River Camp, South Luangwa National Park For an authentic camping experience, **Luangwa River Camp** offers a traditional safari-style camp along the banks of the **Luangwa River**. With tented camps set under towering trees and a variety of game-viewing options, this camp is ideal for those looking for a simple yet immersive adventure.

Key Features:

- **Basic camping** with spacious tents and comfortable bedding.
- **Walking safaris** and **night game drives**.
- Positioned in an area with high wildlife concentrations, ideal for **animal sightings**.

Busanga Plains Camp, Kafue National Park Situated in the remote **Busanga Plains** of **Kafue**

National Park, this luxury camping experience allows guests to stay in tented accommodations equipped with comfortable furnishings and en-suite bathrooms. The camp emphasizes environmental sustainability and offers fantastic opportunities for wildlife viewing.

Key Features:

- **Tented accommodations** with full amenities.
- Access to **exclusive game viewing** in the **Busanga Plains**.
- Offers both **day** and **night safaris** for a full adventure.

Zambezi River Camping, Lower Zambezi National Park For those who want a more basic and adventurous camping experience, **Zambezi River Camping** offers riverside campsites with a direct view of the **Zambezi River**. This no-frills camping experience focuses on connecting with nature and enjoying wildlife sightings in a tranquil environment.

Key Features:

- **Riverside camping** near Lower Zambezi National Park.
- Perfect for **backpackers** and those seeking an **affordable** adventure.
- **Game drives**, canoeing, and **birdwatching** in a peaceful setting.

3. Cultural Lodging: Immersing in Zambian Traditions

Cultural lodges provide visitors with an authentic Zambian experience, where they can stay in traditional-style accommodations, interact with local communities, and learn about Zambia's rich cultural heritage. These lodges celebrate Zambia's diverse ethnic groups, local customs, and historical traditions, offering guests a deeper connection with the country.

Notable Cultural Lodges:

Mukambi Safari Lodge, Kafue National Park While **Mukambi Safari Lodge** offers a mix of luxury and cultural experiences, it is its connection to Zambian culture that makes it unique. The lodge is known for hosting **traditional dance performances**, **cultural storytelling**, and offering **Zambian cooking classes**. It's a great way to experience both safari and cultural immersion.

Key Features:

- **Cultural activities** like **traditional dance performances** and cooking classes.
- Combination of luxury and culture with spacious lodges and tented accommodation.
- Game drives, bush walks, and **local village visits**.

The Toka Leya Camp, Livingstone Located near **Victoria Falls**, **Toka Leya Camp** offers an incredible cultural experience by combining a luxury lodge with local Zambian culture. Guests can explore the **Toka Leya Village**, meet local artisans, and learn about the traditions and crafts of the **Lozi people**.

Key Features:

- Cultural immersion through **community interactions** and village tours.
- **Traditional crafts** and artisan markets.
- Close to **Victoria Falls** with eco-friendly and luxurious accommodations.

Kafue River Lodge, Kafue National Park This eco-lodge blends nature and culture, offering cultural performances and the chance to experience Zambian life through art, music, and storytelling. Guests can also take part in **local farming activities** and enjoy meals made from locally sourced ingredients.

Key Features:

- Immersive cultural activities and **community involvement**.
- **Local cuisine** served with traditional Zambian flavors.
- Situated near **Kafue National Park**, ideal for wildlife viewing and community experiences.

Zambia's unique stays—from **eco-lodges** and **camping** to **cultural lodging**—offer travelers the opportunity to connect with nature and experience the country's rich cultural heritage. Whether you prefer staying in a luxury tented camp in a remote national park, camping by the Zambezi River, or engaging with local communities at a cultural lodge, Zambia provides a wide range of unforgettable and sustainable accommodation options. These experiences allow you to create lasting memories while supporting eco-tourism and cultural preservation in the heart of Africa.

Top Hotels in Zambia: Royal Livingstone, InterContinental Lusaka, and More

Zambia is home to some of Africa's most luxurious and well-renowned hotels, offering a blend of comfort, elegance, and convenience. From the iconic **Royal Livingstone Hotel** near **Victoria Falls** to the business-ready **InterContinental Lusaka**, these top-tier hotels provide exceptional services, stunning views, and a memorable experience for every type of traveler.

1. Royal Livingstone Hotel by Anantara, Livingstone

Located just a stone's throw from **Victoria Falls**, the **Royal Livingstone Hotel** is a 5-star property that offers an unmatched experience of luxury and exclusivity. Situated on the banks of the **Zambezi River**, the hotel provides breathtaking views of the river and the falls, making it one of Zambia's most prestigious places to stay.

Key Features:

- **Direct access to Victoria Falls.**
- **Stunning riverfront views** from rooms and public spaces.
- Spacious rooms and suites with **elegant décor** and modern amenities.
- **Fine dining options** and a world-class spa.
- Exclusive **safari experiences** and access to a variety of adventure activities.

Perfect For: Those looking to combine luxury with adventure, especially those wishing to visit **Victoria Falls** and engage in activities like bungee jumping, helicopter tours, and boat cruises.

2. InterContinental Lusaka, Lusaka

Located in Zambia's bustling capital city, **InterContinental Lusaka** is an ideal choice for both business and leisure travelers. The hotel combines modern elegance with convenient amenities, making it one of the top choices for visitors to Lusaka. With its central location, it offers easy access to government offices, shopping centers, and cultural attractions.

Key Features:

- **Well-appointed rooms** with panoramic views of the city.

- **Business center** and state-of-the-art meeting facilities.
- **Outdoor pool**, fitness center, and a choice of restaurants serving both international and local cuisines.
- **24-hour concierge service** and spacious meeting rooms for business travelers.

Perfect For: Business travelers, conference attendees, and those exploring Lusaka's cultural scene or enjoying the city's vibrant nightlife.

3. The Zambezi Sun Hotel, Livingstone

Located within the same complex as the **Royal Livingstone Hotel**, the **Zambezi Sun Hotel** offers a more affordable yet luxurious stay in **Livingstone**. Positioned near **Victoria Falls**, this hotel offers stunning views of the falls and lush landscapes, with rooms designed in an African-inspired style. It's an excellent option for families and tourists looking for a balance of comfort and value.

Key Features:

- **Proximity to Victoria Falls** and other attractions.

- **Family-friendly accommodations**, including spacious suites and kid-friendly activities.
- **Outdoor pool** and fitness center.
- Several dining options, including a **buffet** and à la carte menus.
- **Cultural experiences** and easy access to safari activities.

Perfect For: Families, adventure seekers, and tourists visiting **Livingstone** for **Victoria Falls**.

4. The David Livingstone Safari Lodge & Spa, Livingstone

For a more secluded and serene experience, **The David Livingstone Safari Lodge & Spa** offers a beautiful riverside location along the **Zambezi River**. This lodge combines luxurious accommodations with incredible views, a relaxing atmosphere, and easy access to nearby **Victoria Falls** and local wildlife reserves.

Key Features:

- Rooms with **private balconies** overlooking the Zambezi River.
- A **full-service spa** offering a variety of treatments and therapies.

- **Lounge and dining** areas with local Zambian flavors and international dishes.
- Proximity to **Victoria Falls** and a variety of **safari experiences**.

Perfect For: Couples, honeymooners, and those seeking relaxation amidst nature while exploring the wonders of **Victoria Falls**.

5. Radisson Blu Hotel, Lusaka

A luxurious property in the heart of Lusaka, **Radisson Blu Hotel** offers modern accommodations for both business and leisure travelers. The hotel is known for its contemporary design, excellent service, and range of amenities. It is ideal for guests who prefer convenience and comfort while staying in the city.

Key Features:

- **Contemporary rooms** and suites with modern amenities.
- **Fitness center**, **spa**, and **indoor pool**.
- A selection of dining options including international cuisine and **local specialties**.
- **Event facilities** including meeting rooms and conference spaces.

- **Airport shuttle** and proximity to Lusaka's commercial districts.

Perfect For: Business professionals, those on a city break, or anyone who appreciates high-end amenities with easy access to Lusaka's business and cultural centers.

6. Lilayi Lodge, Lusaka

For those looking to combine a luxurious stay with an authentic safari experience in Lusaka, **Lilayi Lodge** offers an exclusive, boutique getaway. Set within a 650-hectare game reserve, the lodge offers a unique blend of nature, wildlife, and luxury.

Key Features:

- **Game drives** within the property's private reserve.
- **Charming chalets** with traditional African decor.
- An on-site **restaurant** serving locally inspired meals.
- **Guided walking safaris** and bush experiences.
- **Spa treatments** and a focus on relaxation and rejuvenation.

Perfect For: Nature lovers, those seeking a peaceful retreat, and guests looking to combine luxury with wildlife viewing in Lusaka.

7. Protea Hotel by Marriott Lusaka

For a more budget-conscious yet comfortable stay in **Lusaka**, the **Protea Hotel** by Marriott offers an excellent blend of service, affordability, and convenience. Located near key attractions and business hubs in the city, this hotel is a solid option for both short stays and extended visits.

Key Features:

- **Modern rooms** with functional amenities for business travelers.
- **Restaurant and bar** serving continental and local dishes.
- **Outdoor pool** and fitness center.
- Proximity to **shopping malls** and **entertainment venues**.

Perfect For: Budget-conscious travelers, business professionals, and anyone looking for a convenient, well-located hotel in Lusaka.

Zambia boasts a variety of world-class hotels that cater to every type of traveler. From the opulence of **Royal Livingstone Hotel** by Anantara to the modern conveniences of **InterContinental Lusaka**, each property offers its unique appeal, whether you're exploring the wonders of **Victoria Falls**, on a business trip in **Lusaka**, or seeking a tranquil getaway. These hotels provide not just a place to stay, but a chance to immerse yourself in Zambia's natural beauty and vibrant culture.

CHAPTER FIVE

Practical Travel Information

Transportation: Getting Around Zambia

Navigating Zambia is an adventure in itself, offering a variety of transportation options that range from modern air travel to more traditional methods like buses and taxis. Whether you are exploring the vibrant cities, venturing into the wilds of national parks, or heading to remote cultural sites, understanding the transportation landscape in Zambia will help you make the most of your journey.

1. Domestic Flights: Connecting Zambia's Major Cities and Attractions

Zambia has a well-developed domestic flight network, with several airlines offering flights between major cities and key tourist destinations. Air travel is often the most efficient way to cover long distances, especially if you're heading to remote areas like **South Luangwa National Park**, **Lower Zambezi**, or **Livingstone**.

Key Airlines:

- **Proflight Zambia**: The country's leading domestic carrier, offering flights to cities such as **Lusaka**, **Livingstone**, **Ndola**, **Mfuwe**, and **Solwezi**.
- **Air Zambia**: Provides domestic flights to key destinations including **Lusaka** and **Livingstone**.
- **Fly Zambezi**: Serves regional routes connecting Zambia with destinations like **Johannesburg** (South Africa) and **Harare** (Zimbabwe).

Benefits:

- Quick and efficient travel between cities and major tourist hubs.
- Scenic views, especially when flying over national parks or the **Zambezi River**.
- Regular flights for easier scheduling.

Perfect For: Those looking to save time and reach remote locations, such as national parks, in a shorter time frame.

2. Road Travel: Buses, Taxis, and Car Rentals

For most travelers, getting around Zambia by road is a common choice. The road network in Zambia is fairly extensive, although some areas, particularly in rural regions, can be less accessible. Depending on your destination and travel preferences, options range from long-distance buses to taxis and private car rentals.

Buses:

Buses are one of the most affordable ways to travel between cities and towns. Long-distance buses are readily available and provide an efficient means of travel, especially for tourists on a budget.

Key Bus Companies:

- **Skyways**: Offers travel between **Lusaka**, **Livingstone**, and **Kitwe**.
- **Mazhandu Family Bus Services**: Connects major cities and towns.
- **Eagle Express**: A luxury bus service with air-conditioned coaches and regular routes to key destinations.

Benefits:

- Affordable, especially for budget-conscious travelers.
- Access to both urban and remote areas of Zambia.
- **Comfortable and air-conditioned** options for longer journeys.

Perfect For: Budget travelers, solo explorers, and those planning to travel overland to Zambia's main towns.

Taxis:

Taxis are available in most major cities and are a good option for short-distance travel within urban areas or to destinations within the city limits. However, be sure to agree on the fare before setting off, as meters are rarely used.

Benefits:

- Convenient for city-to-city or short local trips.
- Can be booked in advance or hailed from street corners.
- **Private rides** that are ideal for small groups or solo travelers.

Perfect For: Visitors staying in major cities like **Lusaka** or **Livingstone** who need quick transportation.

Car Rentals:

Renting a car is a popular option for travelers who prefer flexibility and wish to explore Zambia at their own pace. International car rental companies such as **Avis**, **Hertz**, and **Budget** operate in Zambia, alongside local agencies that provide 4x4 vehicles suitable for safaris or rural travel.

Benefits:

- Ideal for self-guided exploration, particularly in remote areas.
- Freedom to visit **national parks** and **remote towns**.
- Access to a variety of vehicles, including 4x4s for **safari trips**.

Perfect For: Independent travelers or those exploring national parks like **South Luangwa** or **Kafue**.

3. Rail Travel: A Scenic and Historical Option

Zambia's rail network is relatively underused by tourists, but it remains a unique and charming way to travel across the country, especially for those with a sense of adventure. The train services are primarily operated by **Zambia Railways**, and the trains run between cities like **Lusaka**, **Kabwe**, and **Livingstone**.

Benefits:

- A **scenic** and leisurely way to travel.
- Less expensive than flights, with the added benefit of meeting locals.
- Ideal for travelers looking for a more nostalgic, slow-paced journey.

Perfect For: Those seeking a different mode of travel and the opportunity to meet locals or enjoy the scenery.

4. Boat Travel: On the Zambezi River

Boat transport is a popular option for tourists looking to explore Zambia's **rivers**, particularly the **Zambezi River**. Boat trips are available for sightseeing, fishing, and even transportation to some remote areas like **Lower Zambezi National Park**.

Popular Boat Services:

- **Zambezi River Cruises**: These boat cruises are a popular activity near **Victoria Falls** and **Livingstone**. Visitors can enjoy **safaris** on the river or take a **sunset cruise**.
- **Safari boats**: Used in national parks for wildlife viewing, particularly in the **Lower Zambezi** and **Kafue** regions.

Benefits:

- Unique, scenic method of transportation, with opportunities for wildlife sightings.
- Relaxing and enjoyable, especially for sightseeing or leisure travel.
- Access to areas where land travel is difficult.

Perfect For: Travelers who want to explore Zambia's rivers, wildlife, and tranquil surroundings.

5. Air Charters: For Remote Areas and Private Journeys

For those visiting Zambia's more remote and less accessible areas, private **air charters** are an excellent option. Many safari lodges and tour operators provide charter flights to **national parks** or secluded areas that are not serviced by commercial airlines.

Benefits:

- Quick access to remote locations such as **South Luangwa** or **Lower Zambezi**.
- The option to travel on your own schedule.
- Scenic flights providing an aerial view of Zambia's natural beauty.

Perfect For: High-end travelers, safari-goers, or those with limited time who want to explore Zambia's wilderness areas.

Getting around Zambia is both straightforward and flexible, with options for every type of traveler. For long distances and remote areas, **domestic flights** and **air charters** are efficient choices, while **road travel** via buses, taxis, or rental cars offers a more immersive, overland experience. For scenic or unique journeys, **boat**

travel and **train rides** provide memorable alternatives. Whatever your mode of transportation, Zambia's roads, rivers, and skies offer exciting ways to explore its vast landscapes, wildlife, and culture.

Currency, Banks, and ATMs

Understanding Zambia's currency system, banking options, and availability of ATMs is crucial for a smooth and stress-free trip. Whether you're budgeting for your stay, handling payments for services, or preparing for an adventure in the wild, this guide will help you navigate Zambia's financial landscape.

1. Currency: The Zambian Kwacha (ZMW)

The official currency of Zambia is the **Zambian Kwacha (ZMW)**. The currency symbol for the Kwacha is **K**, and it is divided into 100 **ngwee** (ngw). The Kwacha is widely accepted across Zambia, from major cities like **Lusaka** and **Livingstone** to more remote areas.

Currency Denominations:

- **Coins**: 1, 5, 10, 50 ngwee, and 1 Kwacha.
- **Banknotes**: 10, 20, 50, 100, and 200 Kwacha.

Currency Exchange:

- **Currency exchange** is available at banks, exchange bureaus, and some hotels. **Foreign exchange rates** fluctuate regularly, so it's advisable to compare rates before exchanging money.
- **US Dollars** are widely accepted for payments in **tourist areas**, but you will need to exchange them for Kwacha if you plan to pay for most goods and services in Zambia.

2. Banks in Zambia

Zambia has a solid banking infrastructure with both local and international banks offering services throughout the country. Most major cities, such as **Lusaka**, **Livingstone**, and **Kitwe**, have a wide variety of banks, while smaller towns and remote areas may have limited options.

Major Banks in Zambia:

- **Zanaco** (Zambia National Commercial Bank): One of Zambia's largest and most widely accessible banks, offering ATMs, branches, and foreign exchange services.
- **Standard Chartered Bank Zambia**: A branch of the international bank, providing comprehensive banking services, including currency exchange.
- **Barclays Bank Zambia**: Another prominent bank with services for travelers, including international money transfers and ATM withdrawals.
- **FNB Zambia** (First National Bank): Known for their convenient services and global banking connections.
- **Ecobank Zambia**: Offers a range of services for travelers, including easy access to international funds.

Banking Hours:

- **Monday to Friday**: 08:00 AM to 03:00 PM.
- **Saturday**: 08:00 AM to 12:00 PM.
- Most banks are closed on Sundays, but some ATMs are available 24/7.

3. ATMs and Cash Withdrawals

ATMs are widely available in urban areas and tourist hotspots. They are a convenient way to withdraw local currency (Kwacha) using international debit or credit cards. Major banks and international financial institutions operate ATMs throughout Zambia, especially in **Lusaka**, **Livingstone**, **Kitwe**, and **Ndola**.

Using ATMs in Zambia:

- **International Card Compatibility**: Most ATMs in Zambia accept **Visa**, **Mastercard**, and **American Express** cards, but it's always advisable to check with your bank about fees and foreign card compatibility.
- **Withdrawal Limits**: ATM withdrawal limits vary, depending on your bank and the type of account. Be prepared for limits on the amount of cash you can take out per day.
- **Currency Options**: ATMs dispense **Zambian Kwacha** only, so ensure you have enough local currency for smaller purchases, especially in remote regions.

Fees and Charges:

- Be aware of potential **ATM withdrawal fees** from both your local bank and the bank operating the ATM.
- Foreign cardholders may also be charged **international transaction fees**, so it's a good idea to check the costs with your bank in advance.

4. Currency Exchange Services

If you need to exchange foreign currency (such as US Dollars, Euros, or British Pounds) to Zambian Kwacha, there are various options available.

Currency Exchange Locations:

- **Banks**: Most banks in Zambia offer currency exchange services at competitive rates. It's recommended to exchange your money at reputable banks to avoid unfavorable rates.
- **Currency Exchange Bureaus**: These are found in major tourist cities like **Lusaka** and **Livingstone**. Exchange rates may vary slightly, but they often offer convenience and faster transactions.
- **Hotels**: Some hotels may provide currency exchange services, but rates may not be as

competitive as those found at banks or currency exchange bureaus.

Tips for Currency Exchange:

- **Exchange in Larger Amounts**: Exchange larger sums at once if possible to avoid additional fees and poor exchange rates when making multiple small exchanges.
- **Avoid Street Vendors**: While it may be tempting, exchanging money through street vendors or informal exchanges can carry risks of fraud and unfavorable rates.
- **Carry Smaller Denominations**: When traveling to remote areas, try to carry smaller denominations of **Kwacha** for easier transactions, as some places may not be able to provide change for large notes.

5. Credit and Debit Cards

Credit and debit cards are accepted at major hotels, upscale restaurants, international shops, and larger retail outlets in **Lusaka**, **Livingstone**, and other key cities. However, **smaller shops** and **markets** may not accept cards, and you will likely need cash for everyday purchases.

Visa and Mastercard:

- Most businesses, especially in **urban areas**, accept **Visa** and **Mastercard**. Ensure that your card has an international capability (most do).
- Some businesses may charge an additional **card payment fee** to cover transaction costs.

American Express:

- **American Express** is less widely accepted than **Visa** and **Mastercard**, but major hotels and certain high-end establishments may accept it.

Tips:

- **Notify your bank** before traveling to Zambia to avoid any issues with card payments or fraud alerts.
- **Carry a backup card** in case your primary card is lost or blocked.
- Keep a close eye on your transactions to avoid unexpected charges, particularly when paying in local currency.

6. Tipping and Payments

Tipping in Zambia is customary but not mandatory. Here's a quick breakdown of what you can expect when tipping:

- **Restaurants**: A 10-15% tip is appreciated in more formal restaurants, though it is usually not added to the bill.
- **Taxis**: Rounding up the fare is common practice.
- **Hotel Staff**: A small tip for housekeeping and bellboys (5-10 Kwacha) is appreciated.

While tipping is encouraged, **cash payments** in **Kwacha** are expected in most places, especially for services like taxis, smaller accommodations, and local businesses.

Understanding Zambia's currency, banking options, and available ATM services is key to a smooth and stress-free trip. While international credit cards are accepted in major tourist areas, having local **Kwacha** on hand is crucial for day-to-day transactions, particularly in rural or less-developed areas. By planning your currency needs and using the available banking infrastructure, you'll be well-equipped to manage your finances and enjoy your time exploring Zambia's many adventures.

Car Rentals and Driving Tips

Exploring Zambia by car offers flexibility, freedom, and the chance to discover the country's stunning landscapes at your own pace. Whether you're venturing into **Victoria Falls**, exploring **South Luangwa National Park**, or heading to remote villages, renting a car provides an excellent way to travel. However, understanding the car rental process, road conditions, and driving tips will ensure a safe and enjoyable experience.

1. Car Rentals in Zambia: What You Need to Know

Car rentals are widely available in Zambia, especially in major cities like **Lusaka**, **Livingstone**, and **Ndola**. Renting a car can be a convenient and efficient way to explore Zambia, particularly for those wishing to visit multiple destinations or remote locations.

Popular Car Rental Agencies:

- **Avis Zambia**: One of the international car rental agencies with offices in **Lusaka** and **Livingstone**, offering a range of vehicles, including **4x4s** for safaris and **compact cars** for urban travel.
- **Budget Rent a Car**: Offers a selection of vehicles and locations for rentals, including **Livingstone** and **Lusaka**.
- **Europcar Zambia**: Another reliable international option, offering well-maintained cars for short and long-term rentals.
- **Zambezi Car Hire**: A local agency that offers both budget and mid-range car rentals, including safari-ready vehicles.
- **Roadtrip Zambia**: Specializes in providing **4x4 vehicles** and **off-road** cars, ideal for those planning to explore national parks and remote areas.

Rental Vehicle Types:

- **Standard Cars**: Ideal for city driving or paved roads.
- **4x4 SUVs**: Perfect for exploring Zambia's national parks, especially **Kafue** and **South Luangwa**, which often require rugged vehicles.

- **Minivans/People Carriers**: Suitable for families or larger groups traveling together.
- **Luxury Cars**: Available at higher-end agencies for those seeking comfort during their travels.

Rental Requirements:

- **Driver's License**: An international driver's permit (IDP) or a valid local driving license from your home country is typically required. Ensure that your license is in English or accompanied by a certified translation.
- **Age**: The minimum rental age is usually 21 years, though some agencies may have a minimum age of 25 for certain vehicles.
- **Deposit**: Rental agencies will typically ask for a **security deposit**, which can be refunded upon the return of the vehicle in good condition.
- **Insurance**: Rental prices often include **basic insurance**, but additional **collision damage waiver (CDW)** and **third-party liability insurance** can be added for extra protection.

2. Road Conditions in Zambia

Zambia's road network is generally well-developed in urban areas, but conditions can vary significantly outside major cities, especially in remote regions or rural areas. Here's a breakdown of the road types you can expect:

Urban Roads:

- Major cities like **Lusaka**, **Livingstone**, and **Kitwe** have paved and well-maintained roads.
- Traffic congestion can be a challenge, particularly during peak hours in **Lusaka**, so be prepared for delays in city centers.

Highways and Main Roads:

- **Paved highways** connect major cities and tourist spots, such as the route from **Lusaka** to **Livingstone** and the **Victoria Falls** area.
- Main roads between **Lusaka** and other urban centers like **Ndola**, **Chingola**, and **Kitwe** are typically in good condition, though potholes and roadworks can occur.

Rural and Remote Roads:

- **Gravel roads** are common in national parks and rural areas. Be cautious on these roads,

especially during the rainy season (November to April), when they can become slippery and difficult to navigate.
- **Off-road driving** is common in national parks like **South Luangwa** and **Lower Zambezi**, where vehicles are required to travel through more rugged, unpaved terrain. For this, a **4x4** vehicle is recommended.

Flooding During the Rainy Season:

- The **rainy season** (from November to April) can cause local flooding, especially in low-lying areas. During this time, **flood-prone roads** may become impassable, and **bridges** may be temporarily closed. It's advisable to check the weather conditions and road reports before traveling.

3. Driving in Zambia: Key Tips and Road Rules

Driving in Zambia can be a rewarding experience, but it's important to be aware of the rules of the road and local driving customs to ensure safety.

Road Rules:

- **Drive on the Left**: In Zambia, vehicles drive on the **left-hand side of the road**, similar to the UK and other countries in the region.
- **Seat Belts**: Seat belts are mandatory for both drivers and passengers in the front and rear seats.

Speed Limits: The typical speed limits are:

- **Urban areas**: 50 km/h (31 mph)
- **Rural roads**: 80 km/h (50 mph)
- **Highways**: 100 km/h (62 mph)
- **Within parks or wildlife areas**: Lower speed limits to protect animals and avoid accidents.

Driving Permits:

- As mentioned earlier, an international driver's permit (IDP) or an English-language driver's license is required to rent a car in Zambia.

Alcohol Limits:

- **Blood alcohol content (BAC)** limits are strictly enforced. The legal limit is **0.08%**. Driving under the influence can lead to fines, arrest, or even jail time, so it's best to avoid alcohol if you plan to drive.

Road Signs and Signals:

- Zambia uses **standard international road signs**, but rural and remote areas may have less clear signage. Keep an eye out for **road signs** indicating local hazards such as **wildlife crossings** or **sharp curves**.

Animals on the Road:

- **Wildlife** is common, especially in national parks and rural areas. Be prepared to stop for animals crossing the road, including **zebras**, **elephants**, and **wildebeest** in national parks.
- When driving in parks, ensure that you drive at low speeds to avoid accidents with wildlife.

Fuel Availability:

- **Fuel stations** are plentiful in major cities and tourist hotspots, but they may be scarce in more remote regions. Be sure to **fill up** before venturing out on long journeys.

- **Fuel quality** is generally good, but **petrol** and **diesel** may not always be available in certain areas, so check ahead if you're heading to remote locations.

4. Safety and Security While Driving

Driving in Zambia can be safe, but like any other country, it's important to exercise caution.

General Safety Tips:

- **Avoid driving at night**: It's generally safer to avoid driving after dark due to limited street lighting in rural areas and the presence of animals on the roads.
- **Lock doors and secure valuables**: While crime rates are not high in Zambia, always ensure your vehicle is locked when unattended, and avoid leaving valuables in plain sight.
- **Carry a mobile phone**: Make sure your phone is charged and equipped with emergency contact numbers, including that of your car rental agency.

Emergency Services:

- **Roadside assistance**: Rental agencies usually provide emergency breakdown assistance as part of their service. Be sure to confirm this before your trip.

Local emergency numbers:

- **Ambulance**: 991
- **Police**: 991 or 096-416-1023 (for emergencies)

5. Navigation and Directions

- **GPS and Maps**: It's advisable to use a **GPS device** or navigation apps such as **Google Maps** for urban travel and familiar routes. For remote areas, download offline maps or carry a physical map, as internet access may be unreliable in some locations.
- **Signage**: Road signs in Zambia are generally clear in urban areas, but in more remote locations, relying on a local guide or GPS may be necessary.

Renting a car in Zambia opens up a world of exploration, from its bustling cities to its vast wilderness areas. While the roads are generally well-maintained in urban regions, be prepared for more rugged conditions as you venture into national parks or rural areas. By following the local road rules, driving safely, and preparing for different terrain, you'll have the freedom to enjoy Zambia's scenic beauty and rich culture on your terms.

Emergency Contacts and Local Safety Guidelines

Zambia is generally a safe country to visit, but it's always important to be prepared for unforeseen situations. Whether you're navigating the bustling streets of **Lusaka**, exploring **Victoria Falls**, or on a safari in **South Luangwa**, knowing the local emergency contacts and safety guidelines will ensure peace of mind throughout your journey.

1. Emergency Contact Numbers

In the event of an emergency, having access to the right contacts can make all the difference. Below are the essential emergency numbers to save on your phone or note down during your travels in Zambia:

General Emergency Numbers:

- **Ambulance**: 991
- **Police**: 991 or **096-416-1023** (available 24/7)
- **Fire Department**: 993
- **Roadside Assistance** (Rental Car Services): Contact your car rental company for specific

emergency contact details. Most companies offer 24/7 breakdown assistance.

Healthcare Emergency Contacts:

- **Zambia National Public Health Institute**: 095-020-5292
- **Livingstone General Hospital (for emergencies in Livingstone)**: 021-332-0330
- **University Teaching Hospital (Lusaka)**: 021-126-5000
- **Private Clinics**: Many private hospitals and clinics across Zambia also offer emergency services. Some of the well-known private healthcare providers include **Medicare Hospital** (Lusaka) and **Cure Children's Hospital** (Lusaka).

Tourism and Visitor Support:

- **Zambia Tourism Agency (ZTA)**: 021-129-0066 (Lusaka Office)
- **Livingstone Tourism Information Centre**: 021-332-0824

2. Local Safety Guidelines

Zambia is generally safe for travelers, but it's important to stay aware and follow safety guidelines to ensure a secure trip.

General Safety Tips:

- **Avoid walking alone at night**: While Zambia is relatively safe, it's best to avoid walking alone in poorly lit areas after dark, especially in major cities like **Lusaka** and **Livingstone**. Always use a **taxi** or **private transport** after dark.
- **Keep your belongings secure**: Petty theft, including pickpocketing, can occur, particularly in crowded places like markets, bus stations, or tourist attractions. Use a **money belt** or **hidden pouch** for valuables, and be mindful of your surroundings.
- **Don't leave valuables in cars**: Never leave anything valuable visible in your car when parked, especially in public spaces. Always lock your vehicle when unattended.
- **Stay informed about local safety**: Keep an eye on local news for any safety updates, especially regarding political events or protests. Travelers are advised to avoid large public gatherings.

- **Use reputable taxis and transportation services**: Always use **licensed taxis** or **ride-hailing apps** like **Bolt** or **Uber** (available in Lusaka) to avoid unregulated drivers.

Wildlife Safety:

If you're traveling to national parks or areas where wild animals are present, always follow these guidelines:

- **Never approach wild animals**: While they may appear docile, wild animals can be unpredictable. Maintain a safe distance and listen to your guide if on a safari.
- **Remain in your vehicle**: While on safari or in wildlife areas, it's best to remain inside your vehicle unless instructed otherwise by a guide.
- **Observe park rules**: Follow the park rules and regulations at all times. Keep noise to a minimum and don't disturb the wildlife.

Safety During the Rainy Season:

The **rainy season** (November to April) can make some roads in rural areas impassable, leading to accidents or delays. Always check the weather forecast and road conditions, particularly if traveling to remote destinations.

- **Flooding**: Some areas are prone to flooding, so avoid driving through submerged roads or crossing rivers when water levels are high.
- **Avoid flash floods**: If you're caught in heavy rains, seek higher ground and avoid low-lying areas prone to sudden flooding.

3. Health and Medical Safety

Zambia is known for its vast wilderness and national parks, but like all international travel, health precautions should be taken to prevent illness and injury.

Vaccinations:

- **Yellow Fever**: Proof of a **Yellow Fever** vaccination may be required upon entry, especially if you're traveling from a country with a risk of Yellow Fever transmission.
- **Malaria**: Malaria is present in Zambia, especially in rural and **low-altitude** areas. Take **anti-malaria medication** before and during your trip and use **insect repellent** to

prevent mosquito bites. Sleeping under a **mosquito net** is also advised.
- **Other Vaccinations**: Ensure that your routine vaccinations, including **tetanus**, **hepatitis A and B**, **typhoid**, and **measles**, are up-to-date.

Emergency Medical Services:

- In case of illness or injury, immediate medical attention is available in larger cities and towns. **Private hospitals** such as **Medicare Hospital** (Lusaka) and **Cure Children's Hospital** are well-equipped for emergencies.
- In case of an emergency, always call **991** for an ambulance. Hospitals and clinics may also have **English-speaking staff**.

Traveler's Insurance:

It's recommended that travelers have **comprehensive travel insurance** that includes coverage for medical emergencies, evacuation, and potential trip cancellations. Ensure the policy covers **emergency repatriation** should you need to return home due to illness or injury.

4. Theft and Scams: How to Stay Safe

While Zambia is generally safe, it's important to be aware of common scams or theft that could affect travelers. Here's how to protect yourself:

- **Avoid street money changers**: While exchanging currency is common, it's better to use official currency exchange bureaus or banks. Street money changers may offer unfair exchange rates or shortchange you.
- **Be cautious with strangers**: If approached by a friendly local offering unsolicited help, such as a guide or taxi service, be cautious. Always verify their credentials before accepting assistance.
- **Watch out for fake tour operators**: If booking tours, especially safaris or trips to remote locations, only book through reputable and licensed operators to avoid scams.

5. Contact Information for Consular Support

In case of lost passports, serious illness, or other consular issues, contact your home country's embassy or consulate in Zambia.

Embassy Contacts:

- United States Embassy (Lusaka): 021-125-1000, **consularl@state.gov**
- British High Commission (Lusaka): 021-125-6000, **Lusaka.consular@fco.gov.uk**
- Canadian High Commission (Lusaka): 021-125-9000, **LUSKA@international.gc.ca**
- Australian High Commission (Lusaka): 021-126-5299, **Lusaka@dfat.gov.au**

For other nationalities, check the **Zambian Ministry of Foreign Affairs** website for embassy contact details.

Zambia is a beautiful, welcoming country with much to offer tourists, from its wildlife and national parks to vibrant culture and history. By following the local safety guidelines, staying informed, and having emergency contacts on hand, you can ensure that your trip will be enjoyable, rewarding, and, most importantly, safe. Always plan ahead, respect local customs, and be prepared for any unforeseen situations to have the most enriching experience in Zambia.

CHAPTER SIX

Cultural Insights and Local Customs

Zambia's Cultural Etiquette

Zambia is known for its warm and welcoming people, and understanding the country's cultural norms and etiquette will help you connect with locals and enhance your travel experience. Whether you're visiting bustling cities like **Lusaka** or exploring rural villages, being mindful of Zambian traditions, social expectations, and communication styles is essential for respectful and enjoyable interactions. Here's a guide to Zambia's cultural etiquette.

1. Greetings and Social Norms

In Zambia, greetings are an important part of daily life and are seen as a sign of respect. When meeting someone, especially elders, take time to greet properly. A brief, friendly exchange is customary in both formal and informal settings.

Common Greetings:

- **"Hello"**: The common greeting in Zambia is "Hello" or "**How are you?**"
- **"Shani?"**: In some regions, people greet each other with "**Shani?**" which means "How are you?"
- **Handshakes**: A handshake is the most common form of greeting, often accompanied by a slight nod of the head or a smile. It's customary to shake hands with people when you first meet them and before leaving.
- **Zambian handshakes**: Sometimes a handshake is followed by a snap of the fingers (a quick and casual gesture).
- **Handshake etiquette**: Always use your **right hand** for shaking hands, as the left hand is considered impolite in many African cultures.

Respect for Elders:

- **Respect for elders** is deeply ingrained in Zambian culture. It's customary to greet elders first in a group setting and to stand or rise when they enter a room.
- When speaking to elders, it's polite to use **formal titles** such as **Mr.**, **Mrs.**, or **Dr.** when

addressing them, unless they invite you to use their first name.

Addressing People:

- When addressing someone formally, it's best to use their full title and last name, especially in professional or unfamiliar settings. For example, say "**Mr. Banda**" or "**Dr. Mwansa**" until invited to be more informal.
- **Nicknames**: Among friends or close acquaintances, people may use nicknames, but always wait to be invited to use them before doing so.

2. Dress Code and Appearance

Zambians typically dress conservatively, particularly in rural areas. When traveling, it's important to dress respectfully and be aware of local attitudes toward modesty.

Appropriate Dress:

- **Modesty**: Both men and women are encouraged to dress modestly, particularly in rural areas. For women, this often means wearing clothes that cover the shoulders

and knees. Avoid overly revealing clothing such as **short skirts**, **low-cut tops**, or **sleeveless shirts**.
- **Business attire**: In urban areas like **Lusaka** and **Livingstone**, more Western-style clothing is acceptable. Men may wear suits or dress shirts and trousers, while women may wear dresses or skirts, depending on the occasion.
- **Traditional Clothing**: Zambians take pride in their traditional dress, especially during cultural events or festivals. Visitors may be invited to wear **Chitenge fabric** (a colorful wraparound cloth) for special occasions, especially when attending ceremonies or traditional gatherings.

Footwear:

- **Shoes**: In general, shoes are expected to be worn in public spaces, and **flip-flops** are considered more appropriate for the beach or casual settings rather than formal outings.

3. Gift-Giving Etiquette

Gift-giving is a common way of showing appreciation or respect in Zambian culture.

150

However, there are certain expectations to be aware of when presenting gifts.

When to Give Gifts:

- **Hospitality**: If you're invited to someone's home, it's a kind gesture to bring a small gift, especially if you've been invited for a meal. It's seen as a sign of respect and appreciation for the invitation.
- **Special Occasions**: Gifts may also be exchanged during weddings, birthdays, or other special events. In these cases, **food items** or **handmade goods** are common gifts.

Types of Gifts:

- **Appropriate Gifts**: Popular gift choices include food, drinks, flowers, or clothing. When gifting, keep in mind that personal items or luxury items may be seen as overly extravagant, especially in rural areas. Simpler and more practical gifts are appreciated.
- **Avoid Alcohol or Spirits**: Giving alcohol to a stranger or someone you don't know well may not be well received. If you're offering alcohol, make sure you understand the

cultural norms surrounding drinking and consumption in the specific area.

How to Present a Gift:

- **Right Hand**: Always offer or receive gifts with your **right hand**, as the left hand is considered disrespectful in many African cultures.
- **Presentation**: Gifts should ideally be presented with a smile, and you may be expected to open the gift in front of the giver to show appreciation.

4. Table Manners and Dining Etiquette

Food plays a significant role in Zambian culture, and mealtime is often an opportunity for bonding and socializing. While eating, it's important to adhere to some basic dining etiquette to show respect to your hosts.

Dining Etiquette:

- **Sharing Food**: Meals in Zambia are often communal, and it is common for people to share from the same plate or dish. It's seen as a sign of togetherness and community.

- **Using Hands**: In some traditional settings, particularly when eating dishes like **nsima** (a staple maize-based meal), **hands** are used for eating, particularly the **right hand**. If eating with your hands, always make sure your hands are clean before eating.
- **Respecting Elders**: Elders are usually served first, and it is respectful to wait until they have started eating before you begin.
- **Politeness at the Table**: Saying "**Please**" and "**Thank you**" is important. When finishing a meal, it's polite to thank your host, regardless of whether you enjoyed the meal or not.

5. Communication Style and Social Behavior

Zambians are known for their friendly, polite, and respectful communication. Understanding how to engage in conversations and interact with others can go a long way in ensuring positive and respectful exchanges.

Tone and Conversation:

- **Polite and Respectful**: Zambians are generally soft-spoken and polite. Avoid

raising your voice or speaking too loudly, as this may be seen as aggressive or rude.
- **Small Talk**: When conversing with strangers or in casual settings, small talk about topics like **family**, **weather**, and **health** is common.
- **Avoid Controversial Topics**: Politics, religion, or sensitive topics such as tribalism can be sensitive subjects in Zambia. If in doubt, steer clear of these discussions unless you are in a close, familiar setting.

Body Language:

- **Eye Contact**: Direct eye contact is common but should be done respectfully, especially with elders or authority figures. Prolonged or intense eye contact can be considered impolite or confrontational.
- **Personal Space**: Zambians are generally not accustomed to a lot of physical contact in social settings, so maintain an appropriate distance while speaking. **Handshakes** or **hugs** may be used among close friends, but it's best to let the other person initiate this.

6. Respect for Local Traditions and Customs

Zambia has over 70 ethnic groups, each with its own unique customs, language, and traditions. As a visitor, it's important to show respect for the cultural practices and beliefs of different communities.

Traditional Ceremonies:

- Zambia is rich in traditional ceremonies, with events like the **N'cwala Festival** (celebrating the first fruits) and the **Kuomboka Ceremony** (a celebration of the Barotse royal family). If invited to such events, dress appropriately and follow local customs.
- **Photography Etiquette**: Always ask for permission before taking photos of people, especially in rural areas or during ceremonies. Some communities may find it disrespectful to have their pictures taken without consent.

By understanding and adhering to Zambia's cultural etiquette, you'll not only show respect to the local population but also create meaningful connections and enjoy a deeper, more enriching travel experience. Whether you're engaging in conversation, sharing a meal, or attending a traditional ceremony, embracing the local customs will help you have a more immersive and enjoyable stay in Zambia.

Festivals, Traditions, and Social Norms

Zambia is a country rich in cultural diversity, with over 70 ethnic groups, each bringing unique traditions, festivals, and social norms. Understanding these aspects will not only enhance your travel experience but also provide insights into the heart of Zambian culture. Whether you are visiting during a festival or engaging with locals in everyday life, knowing the key traditions and social behaviors will help ensure a respectful and meaningful interaction.

1. Major Festivals and Celebrations

Festivals in Zambia are vibrant, lively, and full of cultural significance. They are an essential part of the Zambian social fabric, with each ethnic group having its own unique celebrations. Here are some of the major festivals that you should consider experiencing during your visit:

Kuomboka Festival (Western Province)

- **When**: April (usually, depending on the rise of the Zambezi River).
- **Where**: Mongu, Western Province.

- **About**: One of Zambia's most famous cultural celebrations, the **Kuomboka Festival** marks the annual migration of the Lozi people, as they move from the floodplain to higher ground. The ceremony involves traditional dances, music, and the symbolic procession of the King (Litunga) in his royal barge. The event celebrates the Lozi culture and is a fascinating experience for visitors interested in Zambia's royal heritage and traditional customs.

N'cwala Festival (Eastern Province)

- **When**: February.
- **Where**: Chipata, Eastern Province.
- **About**: The **N'cwala Festival** celebrates the first fruits of the harvest and honors the ancestral spirits. The Ngoni people, one of Zambia's largest ethnic groups, celebrate the festival with traditional dances, music, and offerings to the gods. The festival is a display of Ngoni culture, with the paramount chief playing a central role. It's an excellent opportunity to witness traditional rituals, music, and dance.

Sungo Festival (Northern Province)

158

- **When**: December.
- **Where**: Kasama, Northern Province.
- **About**: The **Sungo Festival** is a traditional celebration of the Bemba people, one of Zambia's largest ethnic groups. The festival is a time for communal gatherings, dances, feasts, and the honoring of elders. The Sungo festival promotes unity and the strengthening of Bemba culture and traditions. During the event, people come together to celebrate the harvest and demonstrate respect for the spirits of the ancestors.

Zambezi River Festival (Livingstone)

- **When**: August.
- **Where**: Livingstone, Southern Province.
- **About**: This festival celebrates the Zambezi River and the communities that live along its banks. It features performances, traditional music, arts and crafts, and local cuisine. The Zambezi River Festival is an excellent opportunity to experience the cultural diversity of the region, with performances from a variety of ethnic groups, alongside opportunities to explore Livingstone's attractions, including **Victoria Falls**.

Unity Day (National Celebration)

- **When**: October 24th.
- **Where**: Nationwide.
- **About**: **Unity Day** is Zambia's national day, marking the country's independence from British colonial rule in 1964. It is a public holiday celebrated across the country with ceremonies, parades, and performances in major cities and towns. Unity Day is a time to reflect on Zambia's journey as a nation and the importance of unity among the country's diverse ethnic groups.

2. Traditional Customs and Social Norms

Zambia is known for its strong family values, respect for elders, and deep-rooted cultural traditions. Understanding these social norms can help visitors navigate local interactions with sensitivity and respect.

Respect for Elders

- Elders hold an esteemed place in Zambian society, and showing respect to them is crucial. It is customary to greet elders first in a group setting, whether in a home, a village, or a formal gathering. In many

cases, younger people are expected to rise when an elder enters a room, and conversation with elders is conducted with great respect.
- **Title and Address**: It is respectful to address elders using formal titles such as **Mr.**, **Mrs.**, or **Dr.** unless invited to use their first name.

Community and Family-Oriented Culture

- Zambia's culture is deeply rooted in **community** and **family**. It is common for extended families to live close together, and many important decisions are made collectively. Visitors may often find themselves invited into homes for meals or celebrations, and such invitations are taken as an expression of hospitality.
- The concept of **Ubuntu** (I am because we are) is prevalent, emphasizing interconnectedness and mutual respect within the community.

Gender Roles and Etiquette

- **Traditional Gender Roles**: While urban areas may have seen shifts in gender roles, in rural areas, traditional gender roles may still be observed. Women are often expected

to take care of household duties, while men handle matters outside the home. However, women in Zambia have an active role in agriculture, commerce, and even leadership in some regions.
- **Polite Interaction**: When interacting with members of the opposite sex, it is important to be respectful, especially in more conservative or rural areas. Public displays of affection are generally frowned upon, and physical contact between men and women is typically limited to handshakes.

Hospitality and Gift-Giving

- **Hospitality**: Zambians are renowned for their hospitality. If invited to a home, it is customary to bring a small gift such as food or drink, particularly if you are staying for a meal. It's also polite to show appreciation for the meal and to wait for the elder or host to start eating before you begin.
- **Gift-Giving Etiquette**: When offering a gift, it's best to use your **right hand**, as the left hand is considered impolite. Avoid extravagant gifts in rural settings, as this may make your hosts feel uncomfortable.

Eating Etiquette

- **Sharing Meals**: Zambians typically share meals in a communal style. Dishes such as **nsima** (maize porridge) are often served in large bowls, and people eat directly from the same dish. In some areas, it is traditional to eat with your hands, particularly when eating **nsima** or **chikanda** (a root vegetable dish). Always wash your hands before eating, especially if you plan to use your hands.
- **Respectful Eating**: It's respectful to eat with others and to offer food to those around you before serving yourself. If you're invited to a meal, it's a kind gesture to accept, even if you're not particularly hungry.

3. Dance, Music, and Arts in Zambian Culture

Zambian culture is rich in dance, music, and the arts, with each ethnic group having its own unique performances and art forms. Music and dance are integral parts of celebrations and social life.

Traditional Dance

- **Makishi Dance**: This is a traditional dance performed during initiation ceremonies by the **Ngoni** and other ethnic groups. It involves wearing intricate masks and costumes that symbolize various ancestral spirits. The dance is performed to invoke blessings and protection for the community.
- **Bemba Dance**: The **Bemba** people, one of Zambia's largest ethnic groups, are known for their lively and energetic dances, often performed during community gatherings, weddings, and festivals.

Music and Drumming

- Drums play a central role in Zambian music. The rhythms and beats are used during ceremonies, celebrations, and social events. Traditional instruments include **drums**, **xylophones**, **flutes**, and **string instruments**. The **Kalindula** style of music, which combines traditional rhythms with modern influences, is popular in Zambia's urban centers.

4. Religion and Spirituality

Zambia is a predominantly Christian country, but traditional African religions and beliefs continue to influence its social life.

Christianity

- Christianity plays a central role in Zambian society, with many Zambians identifying as Christians. Churches, especially in urban areas, are active in community life, and Sunday services are widely attended.

Traditional Beliefs

- While Christianity is dominant, many Zambians still practice elements of traditional African religions, which often involve **ancestor worship**, **rituals**, and **beliefs in spiritual beings**. These practices vary between regions and communities.

Zambia is a country deeply proud of its cultural heritage, and visitors will find a wealth of festivals, traditions, and social norms that make the country truly unique. By understanding and respecting Zambian culture—through participating in festivals, honoring traditions, and following local social norms—you can enjoy a truly immersive and enriching travel experience.

Language Guide and Communication Tips

Zambia is a multilingual country with over 70 languages spoken across its regions, reflecting its rich cultural diversity. While **English** is the official language, most Zambians speak several indigenous languages, which vary by region. Understanding the basics of communication in Zambia can enhance your travel experience, build stronger connections with locals, and show respect for the country's cultures.

1. Official and Widely Spoken Languages

English

- **Status**: English is the official language of Zambia, used in government, education, and business. It is the primary language of communication in urban areas, especially in cities like **Lusaka** and **Livingstone**.
- **Usage**: English is widely spoken and understood by educated Zambians, and

most signs, official documents, and advertisements are in English.
- **Tip**: While English is understood in most areas, knowing a few words in a local language will always be appreciated.

Indigenous Languages

- **Chinyanja (Nyanja)**: Spoken predominantly in the **Eastern Province** and the capital city, **Lusaka**. It's one of Zambia's most widely spoken languages and is often used for casual greetings and everyday conversation.

Greetings: "**Muli bwanji?**" (How are you?)

Response: "**Bwino**" (Good).

- **Bemba**: Commonly spoken in the **Copperbelt** and **Northern Provinces**, it is one of the most widely understood languages in Zambia. It is also the language of the **Bemba** people, one of Zambia's largest ethnic groups.

Greetings: "**Shani?**" (How are you?)

Response: "**Bwino**" (Good).

- **Lozi**: Spoken in the **Western Province**, particularly around **Mongu**. It is the language of the Lozi people and is used during the **Kuomboka Festival**.

Greetings: "**Wai?**" (How are you?)

Response: "**Eeh, wai**" (I'm fine).

- **Tonga**: Spoken in the **Southern Province**, around **Livingstone** and **Zambezi**.

Greetings: "**Muli shani?**" (How are you?)

Response: "**Bwino**" (Good).

- **Kaonde, Lunda, and Others**: Spoken by smaller groups in specific regions such as the **North-Western** and **Western Provinces**. These languages are rich in cultural history and tradition.

Tip: While it's not necessary to speak all these languages, learning a few common words in Chinyanja or Bemba can help endear you to the locals and make your interactions more pleasant.

2. Common Phrases and Greetings

2.1. Basic Phrases

Here are some essential phrases in **Chinyanja** and **Bemba**, two of the most widely spoken languages in Zambia:

Hello:

- Chinyanja: "**Moni**" (Hello).
- Bemba: "**Shani**" (How are you?).

Good Morning:

- Chinyanja: "**Mwauka bwanji**" (Good morning).
- Bemba: "**Shalenipo**" (Good morning).

Thank You:

- Chinyanja: "**Zikomo**."
- Bemba: "**Natotela**."

Please:

- Chinyanja: "**Chonde**."
- Bemba: "**Twalumba**."

Yes:

- Chinyanja: "**Inde**."
- Bemba: "**Ee**."

No:

- **Chinyanja**: "**Ayi**."
- **Bemba**: "**Awe**."

How Much?:

- **Chinyanja**: "**Kuli chinthu chingati?**"
- **Bemba**: "**Chikupi?**"

Goodbye:

- **Chinyanja**: "**Tionana**" (See you later).
- **Bemba**: "**Twachilamo**" (Goodbye).

3. Communication Etiquette and Tips

Greeting Etiquette

- **Greetings Are Important**: In Zambia, greeting people is a significant part of social interaction. It's customary to greet people when entering a room, whether they are strangers or friends. A handshake is common, especially among men, and sometimes it's followed by a snap of the fingers. If greeting elders, be sure to do so respectfully, often first in a group setting.

- **Avoid Direct Questions**: Asking someone how much they earn, their personal status, or other intrusive questions is considered impolite. Instead, focus on neutral topics like the weather, family, or work.

Use of Titles

- **Respectful Address**: When addressing someone, it's important to use **honorifics** or titles like **Mr.**, **Mrs.**, or **Dr.**, especially when speaking to elders or in formal settings. In casual settings, it's okay to use a person's first name, but only after they invite you to do so.
- **Elders First**: Always greet elders first in any group situation. This is a sign of respect, which is highly valued in Zambian culture.

Body Language

- **Posture and Movement**: In Zambia, standing with arms crossed or slouching can be perceived as rude or indifferent. It is best to maintain an upright posture and use open body language when interacting with others.
- **Eye Contact**: Direct eye contact is important as it shows attentiveness and respect.

However, in some cases, especially with elders or authority figures, prolonged eye contact may be seen as challenging or disrespectful. It's best to balance eye contact with deference.

Avoiding Conflict

- **Politeness and Indirectness**: Zambians tend to avoid direct confrontation or harsh arguments, particularly in public. Disagreements are usually handled privately and with a calm demeanor. It's important to be tactful and diplomatic in communication, especially when addressing issues.
- **Avoid Touching**: In some areas, especially rural ones, physical contact between men and women (other than handshakes) may be considered inappropriate. Public displays of affection are generally not seen as acceptable.

4. Language and Communication in Urban vs. Rural Areas

Urban Areas

In cities like **Lusaka**, **Livingstone**, and **Kitwe**, English is widely spoken, and you'll find that many people are bilingual, speaking both English and one or more indigenous languages. English will be sufficient for most interactions in shops, restaurants, and public offices.

Rural Areas

In rural regions, such as the **Eastern**, **Western**, or **Northern Provinces**, indigenous languages like **Chinyanja**, **Bemba**, and **Lozi** are more commonly spoken, and English may not be as widely understood. Learning a few phrases in the local language can go a long way in building rapport and showing respect for the community's traditions.

5. Tips for Effective Communication

- **Learn Basic Phrases**: Even if you don't become fluent, learning a few basic phrases in Chinyanja or Bemba will make a positive impression. Locals will appreciate your effort to speak their language, even if it's just "hello" or "thank you."
- **Ask for Help**: Zambians are friendly and happy to help. If you don't understand something, don't hesitate to ask for

clarification, whether it's directions or how to pronounce a word correctly.
- **Speak Slowly and Clearly**: While many Zambians are fluent in English, speaking slowly and clearly helps avoid confusion, especially if you're in rural areas where English might not be as widely understood.

Zambia's multilingual nature provides a rich opportunity for visitors to immerse themselves in a variety of languages and dialects. By understanding the basics of local languages, using polite greetings, and respecting social norms, you'll enhance your interactions with locals and gain a deeper appreciation of Zambia's culture.

CHAPTER SEVEN

Sample Itinerary and Travel Planning

7-10 Day Adventure Itinerary

Zambia offers a unique combination of wildlife safaris, rich cultural heritage, and stunning landscapes. From the powerful **Victoria Falls** to the vast national parks, this 7-10 day adventure itinerary will take you through some of the country's most exciting destinations. Whether you're looking for thrilling safaris, cultural experiences, or serene escapes, this itinerary covers it all.

Day 1: Arrival in Lusaka

- **Morning**: Arrive in **Lusaka**, Zambia's capital city. Check-in to your hotel and relax after your flight.
- **Afternoon**: Explore the city center, visiting **Kenneth Kaunda International Airport**, **Levy Mall**, and **Freedom Statue**.

- **Evening**: Enjoy a relaxing dinner at **The Royal Dil** or **The Mugg & Bean** for a local experience.

Day 2: Lusaka to Livingstone

- **Morning**: Take a morning flight from Lusaka to **Livingstone** (approximately 1 hour).
- **Afternoon**: Visit **Victoria Falls**, one of the Seven Natural Wonders of the World. Take a walk along the Zambezi River and enjoy breathtaking views of the falls.
- **Evening**: Watch the sunset over the falls with a **sundowner cruise** on the **Zambezi River**. Enjoy dinner at **The Royal Livingstone Hotel** with views of the falls.

Day 3: Victoria Falls & Adventure Activities

- **Morning**: Experience an **adrenaline-packed adventure** such as bungee jumping, zip-lining, or white-water rafting on the Zambezi River.
- **Afternoon**: Visit the **Livingstone Museum** to learn about the region's history and the exploration of **David Livingstone**.

- **Evening**: Enjoy dinner at **The Boma** for a traditional Zambian cultural experience, featuring local cuisine and performances.

Day 4: Livingstone to South Luangwa National Park

- **Morning**: Take an early morning flight to **South Luangwa National Park** (approximately 1 hour 30 minutes).
- **Afternoon**: Arrive and check-in to your **safari lodge**. After lunch, embark on your first **game drive** in the park. South Luangwa is famous for its large population of **elephants, lions**, and **leopards**.
- **Evening**: Enjoy a **sundowner** at the lodge before a delicious dinner under the stars.

Day 5: South Luangwa National Park Safari

- **Early Morning**: Enjoy a **game drive** or a **walking safari** to observe wildlife up close in their natural habitat. South Luangwa is known for its walking safaris, led by experienced guides.
- **Afternoon**: Relax at your lodge or take a dip in the pool, enjoying the views of the park.

- **Evening**: Embark on an evening game drive to see nocturnal animals, such as **hyenas** and **civets**, in action.

Day 6: South Luangwa to Lower Zambezi National Park

- **Morning**: Take a flight from South Luangwa to **Lower Zambezi National Park** (approximately 1 hour 30 minutes).
- **Afternoon**: Upon arrival, check into your accommodation and enjoy a **game drive** or a **boat safari** on the Zambezi River.
- **Evening**: Experience a **sundowner cruise** while spotting wildlife on the riverbanks. Dinner will be served under the stars.

Day 7: Lower Zambezi National Park

- **Morning**: Early morning **game drive** to spot **buffalo, elephants**, and **wild dogs** in the park's diverse habitats.
- **Afternoon**: Go on a **boat safari** along the Zambezi River, where you can view wildlife from a unique vantage point. **Fishing trips** are also available for those interested.

- **Evening**: Enjoy a delicious bush dinner prepared by the lodge while listening to the sounds of the African wilderness.

Day 8: Lower Zambezi to Kafue National Park

- **Morning**: After breakfast, take a flight to **Kafue National Park** (approximately 1 hour 30 minutes).
- **Afternoon**: Arrive and check-in to your lodge. Enjoy an afternoon game drive through one of Zambia's largest national parks, known for its diverse wildlife, including **giraffes, cheetahs**, and **hippos**.
- **Evening**: Dinner at the lodge, followed by stargazing and relaxing in the tranquil setting of the park.

Day 9: Kafue National Park Safari

- **Morning**: Go on an early morning **game drive** to catch the wildlife at its most active. Kafue is less visited, so you'll experience a more remote, untouched feel.
- **Afternoon**: Take a break at the lodge or enjoy an additional **boat safari** along the

Kafue River, spotting elephants, crocodiles, and various bird species.
- **Evening**: Enjoy a sundowner on a riverbank and dinner at your lodge.

Day 10: Kafue to Lusaka and Departure

- **Morning**: Enjoy a final game drive in the early morning, then head to the airstrip for your flight back to Lusaka.
- **Afternoon**: Depending on your departure time, explore the **Munda Wanga Environmental Park** or do some last-minute shopping at **Arcades Shopping Mall**.
- **Evening**: Depart Lusaka for your next destination or return home.

Additional Options for Extension (For 10+ Day Itinerary)

If you have more time or want to extend your adventure, consider visiting:

- **Lake Tanganyika** for water sports and relaxing on the shores of one of Africa's deepest lakes.

- **Livingstone's Mosi-oa-Tunya National Park**, home to a variety of wildlife and the **Victoria Falls**, for more river-based adventures.

Travel Tips for Your Zambia Adventure

- **Visa**: Ensure you have the correct visa for Zambia, especially if you're planning to visit multiple parks.
- **Health**: Bring malaria prophylaxis and be aware of other health precautions.
- **Packing**: Pack light, breathable clothes for safaris, and include sturdy shoes, a hat, sunscreen, insect repellent, and binoculars for wildlife viewing.
- **Guides**: Always go on guided tours for safety and to learn more about the local wildlife and ecosystems.
- **Money**: Carry a mix of cash and cards, especially for remote areas where card payments may not be accepted.

This itinerary offers a comprehensive Zambian adventure, combining thrilling wildlife safaris, cultural immersion, and stunning landscapes for a truly memorable trip.

Best Times to Visit Zambia

Zambia offers year-round appeal, with different seasons offering unique experiences for travelers. The best time to visit depends on the activities you want to do and the specific regions you plan to explore. Whether you're aiming for thrilling safaris, the majestic Victoria Falls, or cultural exploration, here's a breakdown of the best times to visit Zambia based on the season and activities.

1. Dry Season (May to October): The Best Time for Wildlife Safaris

The **dry season** in Zambia, from **May to October**, is the most popular time to visit, especially for wildlife enthusiasts. During this period, the weather is warm and dry, and wildlife sightings are at their best.

Why Visit During the Dry Season?

- **Optimal Wildlife Viewing**: The **vegetation** is less dense, and animals are more likely to gather around waterholes and rivers, making them easier to spot during game drives and walking safaris.

- **Great Safari Opportunities**: This is the best time to visit **South Luangwa**, **Kafue**, and **Lower Zambezi** National Parks, as the wildlife is abundant and active, and the weather is comfortable for outdoor activities.
- **Victoria Falls**: While the falls are smaller in volume compared to the rainy season, the **dry season** offers excellent opportunities for visiting and experiencing other activities like bungee jumping, rafting, and sunset cruises.

When to Visit During the Dry Season:

- **May to June**: The beginning of the dry season, with fewer crowds. Wildlife is becoming more visible, and the parks are still lush from the rainy season.
- **July to October**: Peak safari season. The parks are drier, and wildlife congregates at waterholes. These months offer the best game-viewing opportunities, especially for **big cats**, **elephants**, and **leopards**.

2. Wet Season (November to April): A Tranquil and Scenic Experience

The **wet season** in Zambia spans **November to April**. While this is considered the "off-peak" season, it still offers great experiences, particularly for those looking for **lush landscapes** and **bird watching**.

Why Visit During the Wet Season?

- **Fewer Tourists**: With fewer tourists, you'll experience more secluded and peaceful national parks and wildlife reserves. Accommodation and activities may also be more affordable during this time.
- **Victoria Falls in Full Flow**: The falls are at their most powerful and impressive during the **wet season** (typically from **February to April**). If you want to see **Mosi-oa-Tunya** (the Smoke That Thunders) in its full glory, this is the ideal time to visit.
- **Bird Watching**: The wet season is a haven for **bird enthusiasts**, as migratory birds arrive and the parks become more vibrant with nesting and new life. Areas like **South Luangwa** and **Kafue** are rich in bird species.
- **Lush Green Landscapes**: The parks and surrounding areas are lush and green, creating stunning scenery for photography and leisurely drives. It's also a great time

for exploring **cultural sites** and local communities.

When to Visit During the Wet Season:

- **November to December**: Early rains create green landscapes, and the wildlife starts to disperse as water is more readily available. It's a good time to visit for a quieter experience and for those interested in **photography** of the lush landscapes.
- **January to March**: This is the peak of the wet season. Victoria Falls is at its fullest, and the **Zambezi River** is flowing powerfully. Game viewing is a bit more challenging due to the thick vegetation, but the birdwatching is phenomenal.
- **April**: The rain begins to taper off, and some parks start to dry out, making it an excellent time for early-season safaris and to witness the green landscapes.

3. Shoulder Season (April and November): A Balance of Benefits

The **shoulder season**, in **April** and **November**, offers a blend of the benefits of both the wet and dry seasons. These months are a great choice for those who want to avoid the peak crowds while still enjoying good weather and wildlife sightings.

Why Visit During the Shoulder Season?

- **Fewer Crowds**: These months offer a more intimate experience in Zambia's national parks. With fewer tourists, you'll get more personal attention from your guide and have a more peaceful safari.
- **Affordable Rates**: Accommodation rates can be more affordable in the shoulder season, making it a good time for budget-conscious travelers.
- **Great for Photography**: Both April and November offer stunning landscapes, with the lush greenery still visible in April and the dry season beginning in November, providing fantastic photo opportunities.

4. Considerations for Specific Destinations

- **Victoria Falls**: If you want to experience the falls in their full grandeur, visit during the wet season (February to April). For a quieter experience and a chance to see the falls from different vantage points, including dry-season activities like walking on the

rocks at the base, the dry season (May to October) is ideal.
- **South Luangwa National Park**: Best visited during the dry season (June to October) for excellent wildlife sightings and safaris. **Walking safaris** are especially popular here during the dry months.
- **Kafue National Park**: Best explored in the dry season (May to October) for game drives. However, the wet season brings a unique charm, with lush landscapes and fewer visitors.
- **Lower Zambezi National Park**: Like Kafue, Lower Zambezi is great year-round, but the dry season offers optimal game viewing along the Zambezi River. The wet season, however, offers a more peaceful visit.

Summary:

- **Best for Wildlife and Safaris**: **May to October** (Dry Season) offers the best conditions for game viewing, with easier access to animals and favorable weather for outdoor activities.
- **Best for Victoria Falls**: **February to April** (Wet Season) is the ideal time to see Victoria Falls in its full, powerful glory.

- **Best for Bird Watching and Green Landscapes: November to March** (Wet Season) is the peak time for bird watching and seeing Zambia's parks in their lush, green state.
- **Best for Seclusion and Photography: April and November** (Shoulder Season) offer a balance of good weather, fewer tourists, and more affordable rates.

No matter when you decide to visit Zambia, it offers unforgettable experiences in nature, culture, and adventure. Choose your travel dates based on what interests you most, and you're sure to have an incredible time.

What to Pack and Health Tips

Packing for Zambia requires a bit of planning, especially if you're visiting its national parks, exploring vibrant cities, or experiencing its unique cultural sites. Here's a comprehensive guide on what to pack and health tips to ensure you have a safe and enjoyable trip.

What to Pack for Zambia:

1. Clothing

- **Lightweight, Breathable Clothing**: Zambia's climate can be quite warm, especially during the dry season (May to October). Pack **light cotton or moisture-wicking clothes** that will keep you comfortable while you're exploring or on safari.
- **Neutral-Colored Clothing**: For safaris, wear **neutral colors** such as khaki, beige, or olive. Bright colors can disturb the wildlife and make it harder to blend into the surroundings.
- **Layering Options**: Even during the dry season, mornings and evenings can be cool,

so bring a **light jacket** or sweater for cooler temperatures.
- **Safari Gear**: A **hat** (wide-brimmed for sun protection), **sunglasses**, and a **scarf or bandana** are essential to protect yourself from the sun and dust.
- **Comfortable Footwear**: **Sturdy walking shoes** for safaris, and **flip-flops** or sandals for more relaxed environments. **Closed-toe shoes** are recommended for walking safaris.
- **Swimwear**: If you're staying in lodges with pools or near the Zambezi River, pack **swimwear** for a refreshing dip.
- **Rain Gear (for Wet Season)**: If visiting during the wet season (November to April), bring a **light waterproof jacket** and **umbrella**, as rain showers can be frequent.

2. Health and Safety Essentials

- **Malaria Medication**: Malaria is a risk in Zambia, so consult your doctor before traveling for **malaria prophylaxis** and to discuss other health precautions.
- **Insect Repellent**: Pack **DEET-based insect repellent** to protect against mosquitoes, especially during the wet season and in areas with standing water.

- **Sunscreen**: **High SPF sunscreen** is crucial due to Zambia's strong sun, especially if you're spending time outdoors.
- **First Aid Kit**: Include basics such as **band-aids, pain relievers, antihistamines, anti-diarrheal medication, antiseptic cream**, and any personal medications.
- **Hydration**: It's easy to become dehydrated in Zambia's warm climate, so always carry a **water bottle** with you and drink plenty of fluids.
- **Vaccinations**: Ensure you're up to date on **routine vaccinations** such as **Hepatitis A and B**, **Typhoid**, and **Yellow Fever** (a vaccination certificate may be required to enter the country). Check with your healthcare provider for other recommended vaccines.

3. Travel Essentials

- **Passport and Visas**: Ensure your **passport** is valid for at least six months from your intended date of departure, and check the visa requirements for your country before travel.
- **Travel Insurance**: It's essential to have comprehensive travel insurance that includes coverage for **medical emergencies**

and **evacuation**, especially for remote safari areas.
- **Camera**: A **good camera** or **smartphone** with extra memory cards and **batteries** is essential for capturing the wildlife and landscapes. A **zoom lens** will help with wildlife photography.
- **Binoculars**: **Binoculars** are a must-have for any safari. They will enhance your wildlife viewing and allow you to get closer to animals from a distance.
- **Flashlight or Headlamp**: Pack a **headlamp** or **flashlight** if you're staying in remote areas, as power outages can occasionally occur.

4. Miscellaneous Items

- **Travel Adapter**: Zambia uses **Type G** power plugs, so bring an appropriate **travel adapter** for your electronics.
- **Ziplock Bags**: Useful for keeping small items like toiletries organized or storing snacks.
- **Notebook and Pen**: For jotting down your thoughts, travel notes, or experiences.
- **Snacks**: If you're heading to remote areas, bring **non-perishable snacks** such as nuts, granola bars, or dried fruit.

Health Tips for Traveling to Zambia:

1. Vaccinations and Health Precautions

- **Yellow Fever**: You may need a **Yellow Fever vaccination** if you're coming from a country with a risk of yellow fever transmission. Be sure to carry your **yellow fever vaccination certificate**.
- **Malaria**: Malaria is present in Zambia, so take **malaria prophylaxis** as prescribed by your doctor, especially if you plan to visit national parks or rural areas. **Anti-malarial medications** like **Malarone**, **Doxycycline**, or **Lariam** are commonly prescribed.
- **Other Vaccines**: In addition to yellow fever and malaria, ensure you're vaccinated for **Typhoid**, **Hepatitis A and B**, and **Tetanus**. Consult your healthcare provider for up-to-date vaccine recommendations.

2. Water and Food Safety

- **Drinking Water**: Stick to **bottled water** or **filtered water** while in Zambia. Avoid drinking water from taps, rivers, or lakes to avoid waterborne diseases.
- **Food**: While Zambia's food is generally safe, be cautious about street food and ensure

your meals are freshly prepared and cooked thoroughly. Avoid eating **uncooked vegetables** unless you're certain they've been washed in clean water.
- **Hand Hygiene**: Use **hand sanitizers** with at least **60% alcohol** and wash your hands regularly to prevent illnesses.

3. Sun Protection

- **Sunscreen**: Use **broad-spectrum sunscreen** with **SPF 30** or higher, especially in the dry season. Apply liberally and often, particularly after swimming or sweating.
- **Hydration**: Zambia's heat can lead to dehydration quickly, so drink plenty of **water** and avoid excessive caffeine or alcohol, which can lead to further dehydration.

4. Insect Protection

- **Mosquitoes**: In addition to malaria, mosquitoes in Zambia can carry other diseases such as **dengue fever**. Use **insect repellent** with **DEET**, wear **long sleeves and pants**, and sleep under a **mosquito net** when staying in more rural areas.

- **Ticks**: If you're hiking or walking in grassy areas, check your body for **ticks**, which can transmit diseases. Wear long pants tucked into socks to reduce your exposure.

5. Emergency Health Care

- **Medical Facilities**: Major cities like **Lusaka** and **Livingstone** have **hospitals** and **clinics**, but remote areas may not have easy access to medical care. Always carry a **medical kit** and any necessary prescription medication.
- **Evacuation Insurance**: If you plan to visit remote areas or engage in high-risk activities like safaris, make sure your **travel insurance** includes coverage for **emergency evacuation** in case of illness or injury.

Summary:

When packing for Zambia, focus on lightweight clothing, sun protection, safari gear, and health essentials like malaria medication and insect repellent. Be prepared for the climate and environment with sturdy shoes, a camera, and a first aid kit. For health precautions, ensure you have the necessary vaccinations, carry water purification tablets, and take steps to stay hydrated and protected from the sun and insects.

By following these packing and health tips, you'll be well-equipped to enjoy a safe, exciting, and memorable adventure in Zambia.

Contact Information for Hotels, Restaurants, and Tourist Assistance

Here's a guide with contact details for some of Zambia's most popular hotels, restaurants, and tourist assistance services, ensuring that you have the necessary contacts to help plan and enjoy your adventure.

Hotels and Lodges in Zambia:

Royal Livingstone Victoria Falls Zambia Hotel by Anantara

- **Location**: Livingstone, near Victoria Falls
- **Phone**: +260 213 320 500
- **Email**: royal.livingstone@anantara.com
- **Website**: www.anantara.com

InterContinental Lusaka

- **Location**: Lusaka
- **Phone**: +260 211 258 888
- **Email**: reservations.iclusaka@ihg.com
- **Website**: www.intercontinental.com

Tongabezi Lodge

- **Location**: Livingstone, near Victoria Falls
- **Phone**: +260 213 321 665
- **Email**: reservations@tongabezi.com
- **Website**: www.tongabezi.com

Chiawa Camp

- **Location**: Lower Zambezi National Park
- **Phone**: +260 212 265 331
- **Email**: info@chiawa.com
- **Website**: www.chiawa.com

Mukambi Safari Lodge

- **Location**: Kafue National Park
- **Phone**: +260 977 712 893
- **Email**: reservations@mukambi.com
- **Website**: www.mukambi.com

Zambezi Sun Hotel

- **Location**: Livingstone, near Victoria Falls
- **Phone**: +260 213 320 400
- **Email**: reservations@suninternational.com
- **Website**: www.suninternational.com

Restaurants in Zambia:

The Cave Restaurant & Wine Bar

- **Location**: Lusaka
- **Phone**: +260 211 256 902
- **Email**: info@thecave.co.zm
- **Website**: www.thecave.co.zm

The Royal Court Restaurant

- **Location**: Lusaka
- **Phone**: +260 211 253 763
- **Email**: info@royalcourtrestaurant.com
- **Website**: www.royalcourtrestaurant.com

The Bantu Restaurant

- **Location**: Lusaka
- **Phone**: +260 977 729 362
- **Email**: info@bantu.com
- **Website**: www.bantu.com

Stanley's Bistro

- **Location**: Livingstone
- **Phone**: +260 213 320 287
- **Email**: info@stanleysbistro.com
- **Website**: www.stanleysbistro.com

Mamma Mia

- **Location**: Lusaka
- **Phone**: +260 211 253 645
- **Email**: info@mammamia.com
- **Website**: www.mammamia.com

Tourist Assistance and Helpdesk:

Zambia Tourism Agency (ZTA)

- **Location**: Lusaka
- **Phone**: +260 211 252 570
- **Email**: info@zambiatourism.com
- **Website**: www.zambiatourism.com

Livingstone Tourism Office

- **Location**: Livingstone
- **Phone**: +260 213 322 417
- **Email**: info@livingstone.com
- **Website**: www.livingstone.com

Zambia Wildlife Authority (ZAWA)

- **Location**: Lusaka
- **Phone**: +260 211 290 496
- **Email**: info@zawa.gov.zm
- **Website**: www.zawa.gov.zm

Tourism Zambia (Local Tour Operator)

- **Location**: Lusaka
- **Phone**: +260 977 763 736
- **Email**: info@tourismzambia.com
- **Website**: www.tourismzambia.com

Zambezi River Authority (Victoria Falls)

- **Location**: Livingstone
- **Phone**: +260 213 320 578
- **Email**: info@zambezira.org
- **Website**: www.zambezira.org

Emergency Contacts:

Zambia Police Service (Emergency)

- **Phone**: 991 (or +260 211 253 643 for non-emergencies)

Emergency Medical Services

- **Phone**: 993

Zambia Red Cross Society

- **Phone**: +260 211 254 906
- **Email**: info@redcross.org.zm
- **Website**: www.redcross.org.zm

Tourist Police (Livingstone)

- **Phone**: +260 213 320 473

Zambia National Tourism Helpdesk (24/7)

- **Phone**: +260 211 252 570

Tips for Reaching Out:

- **Emailing** ahead of time for hotel reservations, activity bookings, or inquiries about Zambia's parks is recommended for convenience.
- **Cell phone roaming** works in most areas of Zambia, but it's advisable to check with your mobile carrier for coverage, especially in more remote regions.
- **Local SIM cards** are available at airports and major towns for cheaper calls and internet.

Having these contacts readily available will help you navigate your trip with ease, ensuring that you can reach out for assistance or make necessary bookings while in Zambia.

Conclusion

Zambia offers a rich tapestry of experiences for travelers, from its awe-inspiring natural wonders like Victoria Falls to its abundant wildlife in South Luangwa and Kafue National Parks. The country's vibrant culture, hospitable people, and diverse landscapes provide a perfect setting for an adventure-filled journey. Whether you're looking for thrilling safaris, serene river cruises, or a taste of authentic Zambian cuisine, this beautiful destination has something for everyone.

By planning ahead with essential travel information—such as accommodations, local dining spots, transportation, and safety guidelines—you'll be well-prepared to explore all that Zambia has to offer. Remember to pack wisely, stay informed about health precautions, and respect the local customs and traditions to ensure a safe and enjoyable trip.

With the resources and tips provided in this guide, you're ready to embark on a memorable Zambian adventure. From the bustling city life of Lusaka to the tranquil retreats near the Zambezi River, Zambia is a destination that promises unforgettable moments, whether you're a first-time visitor or a seasoned traveler. Safe travels and enjoy your adventure in one of Africa's most captivating destinations!

Made in United States
Troutdale, OR
04/28/2025